Illustration Research Methods

BLOOMSBURY VISUAL ARTS
Bloomsbury Publishing Plc, 50 Bedford Square, London, WC1B 3DP, UK
Bloomsbury Publishing Inc, 1359 Broadway, New York, NY 10018, USA
Bloomsbury Publishing Ireland, 29 Earlsfort Terrace, Dublin 2, D02 AY28, Ireland

BLOOMSBURY, BLOOMSBURY VISUAL ARTS and the Diana logo are trademarks of Bloomsbury Publishing Plc

First published in Great Britain 2021
Reprinted 2021, 2023, 2024, 2026

Copyright © Rachel Gannon and Mireille Fauchon, 2021

For legal purposes the Acknowledgements on p. 224 constitute an extension of this copyright page.

Cover design: Angelo Stitz

All rights reserved. No part of this publication may be: i) reproduced or transmitted in any form, electronic or mechanical, including photocopying, recording or by means of any information storage or retrieval system, without prior permission in writing from the publishers; or ii) used or reproduced in any way for the training, development or operation of artificial intelligence (AI) technologies, including generative AI technologies. The rights holders expressly reserve this publication from the text and data mining exception as per Article 4(3) of the Digital Single Market Directive (EU) 2019/790.

Bloomsbury Publishing Plc does not have any control over, or responsibility for, any third-party websites referred to or in this book. All internet addresses given in this book were correct at the time of going to press. The author and publisher regret any inconvenience caused if addresses have changed or sites have ceased to exist, but can accept no responsibility for any such changes.

A catalogue record for this book is available from the British Library.

ISBN PB: 978-1-3500-5143-0
      ePDF: 978-1-3500-5144-7
      eBook: 978-1-3500-5145-4

Typeset by Angelo Stitz
Printed and bound in Great Britain

For product safety related questions contact productsafety@bloomsbury.com.

To find out more about our authors and books visit www.bloomsbury.com and sign up for our newsletters.

Illustration Research Methods

Rachel Gannon and Mireille Fauchon

BLOOMSBURY VISUAL ARTS
LONDON · NEW YORK · OXFORD · NEW DELHI · SYDNEY

1 INTRODUCTION

Defining illustration practice, principles and methods. A framework for researching as an illustrator.

2 ILLUSTRATION RESEARCH

Using narrative theory to analyse how narratives are constructed and communicated. Storytelling as an illustrative research method and how stories function in the 'real world'. Distinctive methods for reading, analysing and interpreting texts as an illustrator and how words and text can be illustration.

3 AUTHORSHIP

Where and how to start researching when working within documentary and journalistic practices. Methods for researching the lived experience of others, including listening and observing, and engaging people and communities through practice. Navigating issues and concerns around authenticity, truth, representation, accountability and positioning.

4 REPORTING

Making as a distinctive research method, where the workshop is a laboratory, and thinking happens through experimentation and prototyping. Understanding materials, tools and objects and how they hold and convey meaning. Applying illustrative thinking and methods to found objects, 3d forms, tactile works and the virtual realm.

CRAFTING

5 ACTIVISM

Why an understanding of political and economic ideas and structures is needed for an informed research practice. Strategies and methods the illustrator can use to 'activate' audiences and disseminate ideas. The illustrator as facilitator and working with people and communities.

137

6 EDUCATION

Pedagogic ideas and methods and how to develop your own distinctive approach or philosophy. Using illustration as a method and an outcome to teach / learn other subjects including creating educational experiences and activities, using storytelling and (self) narrativisation and interactivity, and performative methods.

165

7 ILLUSTRATION FUTURES

Speculative imaginings for illustration as a discipline, practice and method.

203

APPENDIX

Practical advice and useful information for proposals, interviews and working with others. How to ensure a reflective, responsible and ethical approach to research.

207

INTRODUCTION

The ideas in this book have developed over many years. We met as students in 2006, both specialising in illustration on the then named Communication Art and Design MA programme at the Royal College of Art. From that point we formed a co-supportive friendship and went on to become colleagues and collaborators, all the while navigating and negotiating our individual roles as illustrators, practitioners, educators and researchers.

Throughout our professional lives we have fortunately found ourselves working within an expansive community of practice, encompassing creatives, thinkers, makers, educators and theorists, all highly skilled and knowledgeable across a diverse range of specialisms. The critical position at which we find ourselves has, in no small part, been influenced by the generosity of this informative network.

To describe the illustration industry as changing is now somewhat platitudinous. What can be asserted with confidence is that the field is as wide as it is amorphous. No predicted visual, or indeed creative, response, can be expected of the contemporary practitioner. We believe contemporary illustration practice to be at a critical point.

The expansion of illustration practice goes hand in hand with its rise in popularity among prospective students. The educational environment is often where the most exploratory forms of practice are found. What we urgently need to consider is how to foster this ambition in such a way that can translate and have application within an increasingly precarious professional environment. Students can graduate to find a fissure between the reality of a professional practice and the experimental ways of working encouraged in education, and struggle to transfer the skills and knowledge they've gained to work in adjacent fields. This has prompted an irreversible shift towards the formation of a subject no longer confined by parameters set by industry or business. New agendas are fuelled by imagination, inventiveness and yearning aspiration.

Students are consistently the most valuable resource any educator can draw from, and it is here that we look to ascertain what the future might hold for illustration. The students we have worked with have constantly challenged our understanding of the forms that illustration can take and the ways it can operate, and they humbly remind us of our position as facilitators, not connoisseurs.

About this book

The impetus to write this book was born from a recognition that no texts could be found on any generic academic reading lists that captured our burgeoning philosophy of illustration as a discipline. Despite a concerted effort among the international academic community – notably the Illustration Research Network – to establish new benchmarks for the study of illustration, we recognised a serious shortfall in the subject of specific critical discourse. With practice-based research being the mainstay of much of our approach to teaching, we wanted to produce a text that paid particular attention to the mechanisms of illustration. Too often, emphasis of illustration work is placed on the finished artefact, the stylistic decisions made and/or the message conveyed. However, much of our time working with students focuses on developing methods, the processes of thinking and doing, which enable an intelligent and articulate body of work. To advance the subject, what is required is a close analysis of the methods through which it is determined, the means of production and the rigorous processes and considerations that inform the most seemingly miniscule of decisions.

This book attempts to describe the methods we recognise as distinctive within contemporary practice and to acknowledge them, not only as integral to the realisation of an illustration artefact, but intrinsic to the holistic creative outcomes. Rather than dwell on finished products, we address the *hows* and *whys* and analyse the ways in which the most ambitious of illustration practice can operate and perform.

Who can use this book?

This is a practical text written with students, academics, theorists and practicing illustrators in mind. It can be used as a manual for reference, or an aid when guidance or support is needed. It is not a 'how to' guide as there are no 'right' or 'wrong' ways of working. The methods we describe are transferable. They can also be adapted and applied to suit the needs of the individual project at hand. Practice and theory are addressed as one.

Constellations

The structure of the book aims to support individual practices and new ways of working, rather than predetermining a singular approach. Each of the five main chapters (Authorship, Reporting, Crafting, Activism and Educating) explores a different facet of illustration practice.

The titles given to the chapters in this book were assigned very early on in the writing process. They were only ever intended as a loose framework of the key concerns and roles we recognised illustrators being informed by. We had always anticipated that eventually we would arrive at more specific, perhaps poetic, titles, but found that the diversity of practice which we were describing needed a suitably broad umbrella beneath which to shelter. The headings should thus not be understood by their most literal and familiar meanings, but rather be regarded in their broadest application. Different methods and concerns are then clustered around these central tenets, addressing critical ideas, theoretical frameworks, and concerns and questions related to the various motifs.

This book acts as a guide; a map of constellations to encourage the reader to make connections between individual methods that suit their needs and desires, and in doing so, to form distinctive practitioner-specific illustration methodologies.

What is it that you do?

This book is a demonstration for those who wish to commission or collaborate with illustrators but perhaps find the creative process elusive. This text is intended to consecrate links between exploratory educational practices and professional applications in an industry where the ability to communicate with empathy and clarity is a much-desired and sought-after skill. Making known the

INTRODUCTION

What is it that you do?

value of our creative discipline to future employers, collaborators and commissioners outside of the 'bubble' of academic study will ensure our graduates enter a professional landscape where experimental practices are valued and flourish.

Models of practice

This book is foremost concerned with the methods through which illustration is performed, rather than a survey of contemporary practice. Throughout the process of penning this text we have been adamant that a diverse sample of illustration should be included, with emphasis on practices that are particularly experimental, challenging or speculative in nature.

We have never desired to produce a catalogue of exemplary, or historically noteworthy individuals or works. We would not assume the authority to declare the simplistic binary definitions of 'good' or 'bad' illustration. Nor do we claim this as an all-encompassing compendium indicative of all global practices. Such a feat would be impossible. Rather, we have drawn from our experiences working in education where we have found ourselves the most exhilarated and excited for future prospects.

It was decided from the beginning that many of the featured practitioners would be in the early stage of their careers, and equal value would be attributed to student works, self-initiated and commissioned projects.

Not all the works here are strictly illustrative, and by this we mean the producers don't necessarily self-identify as illustrators or define their projects as illustration by intention. These have nevertheless been included because they share common principles and display an ingenuity from which we can learn. We have also included vernacular or incidental works, such as protest posters, that we recognise as operating with illustrative effect.

A NOTE ON ILLUSTRATIONS

A book about illustration must certainly be illustrated. The images featured here serve as illustrative aids for the concepts described in writing, as well as portrayals of illustrative projects in their own right. Within illustration, context is everything; we have therefore endeavoured to use images that are an accurate representation of illustrations in their intended context, where appropriate, unless this hampered readability. In such cases illustrations have been reproduced in insolation.

At times, we have featured multiple images from the same project to give a better flavour of the works in their intended use. As appropriate, and in line with the ethos of this text, we have endeavoured to illuminate methods in process rather than finalised outcomes.

Acknowledgement should be made that illustrations in original context exist with scale, materiality and tactility that no reproduction can imitate completely. These facsimiles cannot replace the human experience of encountering and engaging with these works in their intended environments. Those interested in learning more about these projects are warmly encouraged to extend their investigations and to seek out the comic, print, newspaper, website or film and experience the works for themselves.

TRANSLATIONAL TYPE
Angelo Stitz
A note from the designer

As a designer I am always trying to make the essence of content tangible. This was strongly in mind when I was asked to find my own interpretation of this book's title, *Illustration Research Methods*. For me, illustration stands for a mark: a dot, a line a fragment of human trace that can be read and interpreted. Research is the intention to find meaning in this individual mark. Methods are possible ways to achieve this endeavour.

Readers of this publication become part of this creative process. Each engagement is an individual research process where signs, here letter forms, grow and merge to finally constitute meaning. The transitions and juxtapositions of these signs relate to how this book can be used to support how creative practices are encountered.

I developed a specific typeface, seen on the cover and chapter opening pages, where I broke down each alphabetic character to its stroke fragments, revealing their constituent forms. An alphabetic character is often seen as a closed entity, but deconstruction reveals that most share similarities. Some characters, *E* or *F* for example, share the same fragments, while others such as *S* cannot be broken down further.

All these different forms overlap and merge with the character fragments from the previous line of text to construct new unexpected characters. Furthermore, it allows for a space where new undefined signs are revealed that cannot as yet be read, but are still recognisable as unusual typographic characters.

From my point of view, this is exactly what this book is about. Making connections between processes that at first seem to be isolated. The three words *Illustration Research Methods* separated here just by a blank space, to my mind, can also be translated into *Intuition Exploration Systematics* making clear the tension that exists between these words. Using the words 'intuition' and 'systematic' in the same sentence is almost contradictory. However, I understand this book serves to disprove these oppositions, so original perspectives can be connected, triggering a generative process for the emergence of new artistic practices.

INTRODUCTION

TRANSLATIONAL TYPE
Angelo Stitz

Models of practice

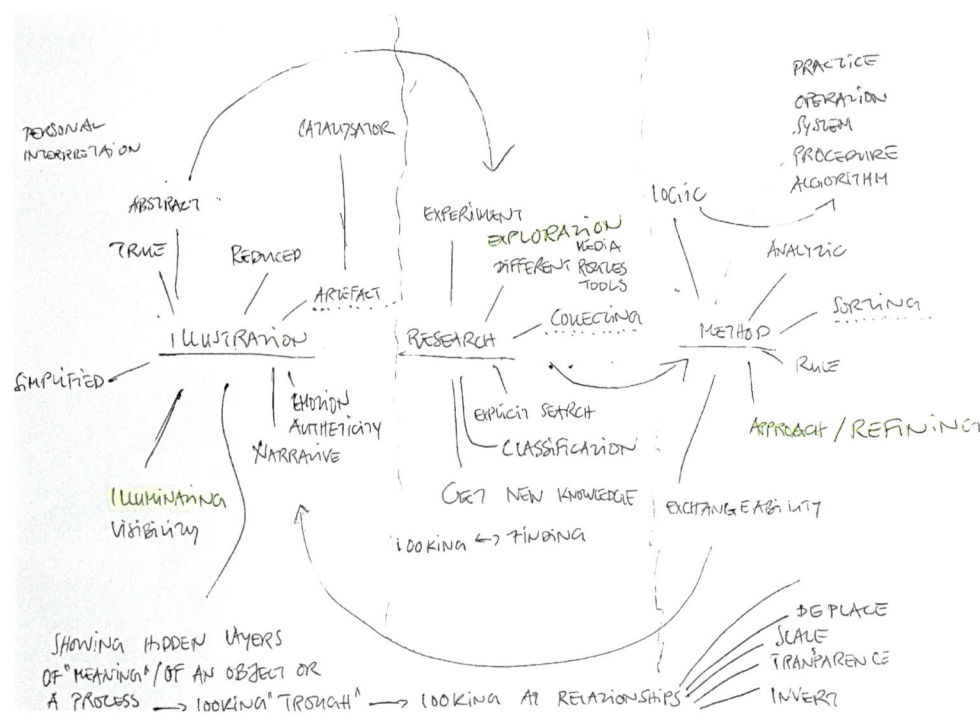

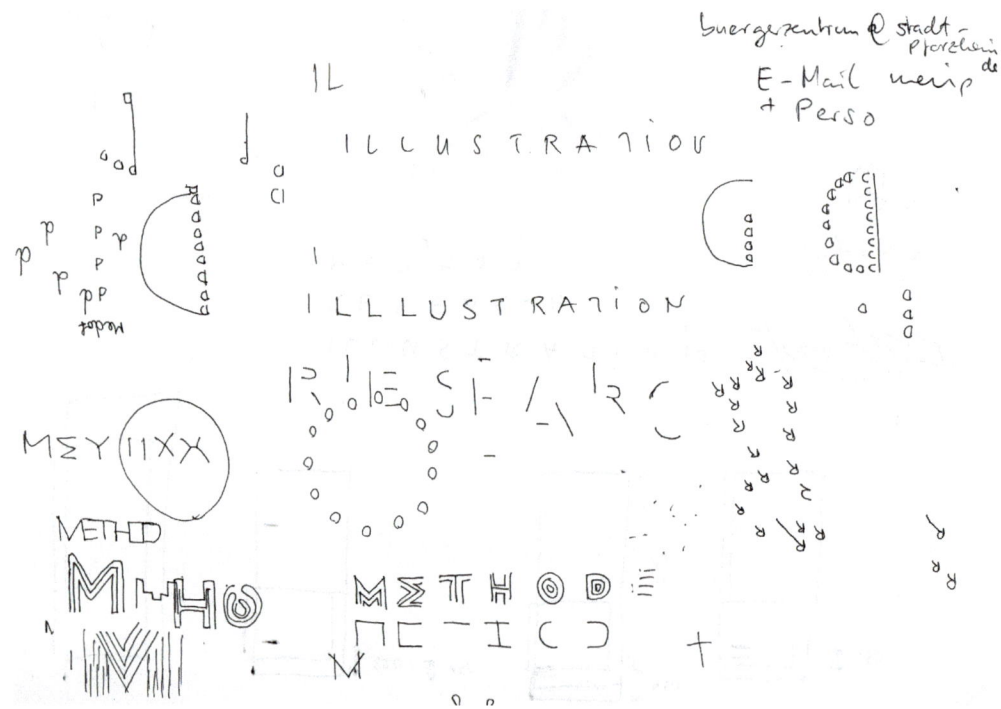

THE LETTER AS DOT

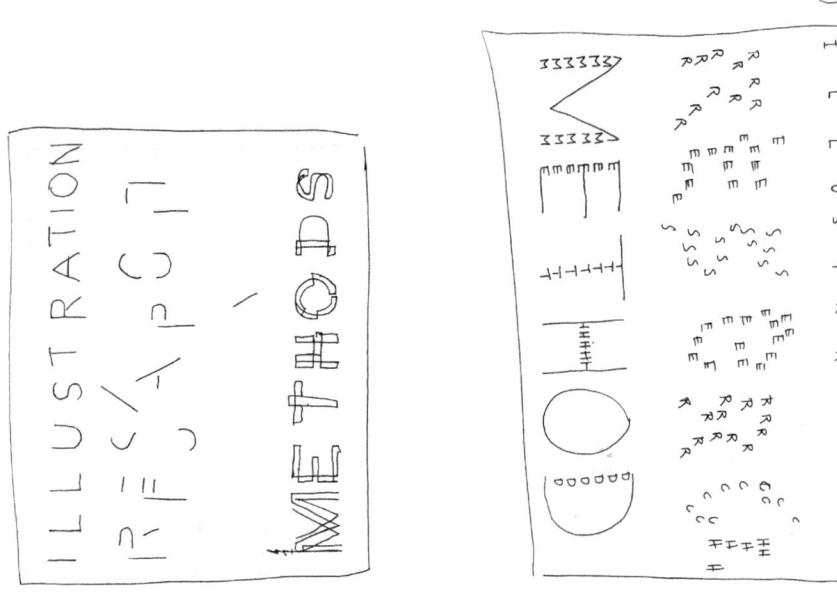

1 ILLUSTRATION RESEARCH

PART 1: ILLUSTRATION

014 — Definitions
— Illustration as process
015 — Identity
— Language and terminology
016 — The principles of illustration practice
017 — Shifting roles – an expanded practice
018 — Can illustration ever be authorless?

PART 2: ILLUSTRATION AND RESEARCH

019 — A social practice
020 — Research into, through and for illustration –
a framework for categorising methods
— Rigour in illustration
022 — Originality in illustration
023 — Endnote

ILLUSTRATION HAS COME TO NOT ONLY DESCRIBE PRACTICE OF CREATIVE MAKING BUT ALSO ONE OF COGNITION, THINKING, AND REASONING.

PART 1: ILLUSTRATION

Illustration is an enthralling discipline. As educators, we have gladly learnt to abandon expectations as year after year we witness practices develop that disrupt with gusto all previous known parameters. Professionally, illustrators are now multifarious beings, positioning their practices to respond to the subject matters *they* recognise as most urgent in the here and now. Illustration has come to not only describe a practice of creative making but also one of cognition, thinking and reasoning, capable of bearing significant theoretical weight. The illustrator's knowledge is not only contained in the hands or in the manipulation of materials, it is also present in their canny perception, acute questioning and empathetic, intersubjective rapport. Illustrative forms and material outcomes refuse to be taken for granted. Practices are now expansive, as illustrators extend and shift their works to assume new roles and responsibilities. No longer is it sufficient to look to the past for reference and rationale. Rather, we must self-determine from within the crucible of a contemporary discipline, and project outwards with earnest and uncompromised ambition.

Definitions

The mandate of this book is not to anchor an all-encompassing definition of illustration, or to claim to exemplify all practices. With a discipline so chimera-like as contemporary illustration practice, such a task would be as futile as it would be thankless. However, it is important to recognise that definitions can offer clarity, a sense of belonging and an acknowledgement of distinction. Distinctions infer specialist knowledge and expertise; they describe a landscape within which we position ourselves while acknowledging a lineage and legacy. 'Illustration' encompasses much more than just visual additions to printed written texts, yet rudimentary dictionary definitions can still be found describing illustration as 'a picture illustrating a book, newspaper' etc. There certainly are forms of illustration that are more familiar and easily determinable, including decorative or representational pictorial images made in response to written sources. Professionally, illustration is also commonly associated as being brief-led and belonging within commissioned dynamics for commercial application within industries such as publishing, advertising, packaging and so on.

As practices emerge that divert, sometimes entirely, from familiar conventions, what is needed is a recognition of the increasing pluralism within illustration, and with it a confident and sophisticated vocabulary through which it can be critically described and examined.

This book claims a terminology designed specifically to articulate the languages and mechanisms through which illustration operates. The content is by no means definitive, but offers a working lexicon with the expectation that it will and should be extended, developed and reformed.

Illustration as process

With discipline-specific critical discourse in its infancy, the methods used by illustrators have never been formally framed in academic language. The absence of a common framework leaves little precedence in guiding discussions of how illustration methods might function and perform. Analysis and critique of illustration is often only concerned with visual outcomes. Outside the educational environment, analysis rarely extends to examining the complex, and often highly individual, methodologies involved in realising works of illustration. When processes are addressed, there can be a tendency to frame the discussion as examples of 'good' vocational practice. Materials and processes can be fetishised, with the figure of the illustrator seen as an elusive genius whose persona, visual style or methods of creation dare not be shared for fear of imitation.

However, if we consider the phrasing 'to illustrate' as an active verb, the illustration outcome or artefact forms just a limited part of a wider process in motion. Furthermore, it presents new questions of how illustration can be applied and commodified. Illustration is typically purchased as an outcome, whether acquired as a service or as an artefact. Might illustrators enjoy new employment opportunities if value was duly placed on the expertise involved in communicating and engaging with targeted audiences? This might involve illustration applied as methodology, or an illustrator engaged professionally as a creative consultant.

Identity

One of the most important factors influencing the future of illustration is giving illustrators the confidence to describe themselves as such. Many of those exploring innovative or expanded notions of illustration choose to adopt more all-encompassing monikers – creative, designer, maker, artist – for lack of a seemingly more suited title. This means those actively engaged in challenging or progressing the discipline remove themselves and their pioneering practices from discipline-specific discussions.

Illustration's versatility has often lead it to be described as interdisciplinary. As with all disciplines, there is no one particular method, form or concern, but this does not mean illustration is inherently interdisciplinary, and to describe it as such can induce feelings of insecurity. Illustration has its own distinctive methods and strategies. These are not, as it were, 'interdisciplinary' as in oscillating between various disciplines, but are particular within illustration. Of course, when practiced with innovation, illustration will look towards and learn from other subjects, but this is not to deny that there are recognisable discipline-specific models.

Language and terminology

Regardless of whether illustration is considered an established or emergent discipline, it has lacked the subject-specific critical eloquence established within other artistic disciplines. While much is gained from engaging in cross-disciplinary discourse, illustration too often looks outside itself for rationalisation and inspiration in the absence of its own intellectual tools. Terminologies and languages are frequently adopted from other fields to articulate illustration-specific behaviours and engagement; for example, illustration is often described as being 'read'.

The development of illustration relies on investment in discipline-specific theory. To neglect this is a failure to recognise the complex processes in operation and to risk illustration being marginalised as a lesser art form. Within this text we have attempted to isolate and describe methods, not appropriated from the other subjects, but those we recognise as being particular to illustration.

Method
: A tool, process or technique utilised to realise a specific aim.

Methodology
: A strategic system or series of methods selected to conduct a sustained inquiry or to perform a task.

The principles of illustration practice

In order to discuss how illustration performs, it is necessary to first offer a working model of the principles of illustration. The following describes the mechanisms we recognise as being commonly operational within illustrative works regardless of their final form, the subject matter addressed or the impetus for the project. The points made here do not claim to be exhaustive, nor do we suggest all works of illustration must concede to all these mandates. Rather, we intend to create a reference in order to aid a shared understanding of why we regard the works we discuss as illustration. This template also allows us to identify and relate those works which are not strictly illustrative as relevant to our inquires.

PRINCIPLES

Social/Public – practices often involve social engagement with people or the public. This may refer to research methods dependent on personally engaging with other creative collaborations or more pragmatic negotiation with professional partners and commissioners. Audience specific – audience reception is considered. Communicative – works that actively seek to engage and be understood. Multiform – illustration is not defined by material boundaries and can manifest in any way, including sculptural, time-dependent or virtual forms. Intent – practices are conscious and informed by motive, even if the knowledge sought or the results gained are initially unknown. For example, intentional practice may be exploratory, diagnostic or convey information.

COMMON STRATEGIES

Narrative – storytelling and narrative as a method of engaging, communicating and/or presenting information and content. Creative interpretation – use of fiction or imagination to extend knowledge and/or relate to and engage with audiences. Participation – works that rely on or incorporate audience engagement in order to be fully realised. Examples of participation could be physical engagement with a work such as reading a publication, a public showcase to gauge reception or involving audiences within activities such as workshops or performances. Participation may occur at any stage within an illustration project. Responsive – illustration methods are responsive and adaptable. Methodologies are tailored to the task at hand, the environment, people and situations that the illustrator is engaged with.

BEHAVIOURS

Subjective – often describing personal or specific viewpoints or positions. Empathic – engaging through use of emotion, e.g. humour, compassion, anxiety, etc. Persuasive – able to inform and influence opinion or decision-making. Provocation – used to prompt consideration or to challenge preconceived notions. Transferability – works that are mobile or adaptable to contexts and audiences, for example, illustration contained or realised in book form are portable; screen-based works can be disseminated via the internet. This is often linked with impermanence and/or widely reproduced ephemeral works. Accessibility – works that are open and/or particularly targeted to diverse audiences. This may be also understood as works that engage groups who are not traditional audiences of the arts and/or may not consider themselves to be engaging with an art form. Accessibility can also be inferred by context, e.g. through operating or being encountered outside of traditional art venues.

TOOLS AND INSTRUMENTS Here, we are not referring to art materials and processes used in the production of illustrative artworks (there is a more expansive discussion of what might constitute a tool within illustration in Chapter 4: Crafting), but rather the tools and instruments that enable and facilitate illustration as a wider discipline. In no particular order of significance, these can be understood as: <u>Organisations and individuals</u> who fund and commission illustration. <u>Venues and platforms</u> that host or showcase illustrative works, such as exhibition spaces, book fairs, online forums, cinemas, etc. <u>Agents</u> who represent illustrators professionally, facilitate the production of illustration projects and liaise professionally on behalf of the illustrator. <u>Organisations</u> who employ illustrators for their professional expertise, for example as consultants, researchers or data visualisers. <u>Retailers</u> who trade in illustrative works and artefacts. <u>Contexts</u> for illustrative art works such as the screen, the page, the poster, the stage set, the fabric sample, etc.

Shifting roles – an expanded practice

In professional practice, illustrators will likely experience different ways of working, as appropriate to the task and their preferences as creative individuals. Self-initiated projects are no longer confined to occupying time and exercising skills between commissions. Illustrators are increasingly autonomous in identifying professional opportunities and actively seeking out markets and contexts for their practices.

Authorial practices, more specifically, place the illustrator in control for the conception and realisation of their projects. Here, the individual dictates the concerns, themes and portrayal of their illustrative content. Such projects may be produced entirely independently and without influence from any external agent.

Authorial and autonomous practices are now far from novel. A 'working' illustrator can expect to find themselves engaged in a variety of projects, often moving across self-directed, commissioned and collaborative projects. As approaches, forms and professional dynamics shift within illustration, disruption is brought to familiar commodity-based, transactional or commissioned relationships. Hierarchies between clients, agents, designers, publishers and indeed among illustrators are being challenged and in some cases, disappearing altogether. Illustrators are proactively establishing expanded practices through which they can broadly apply their skill sets and occupy a number of roles.

Autonomous practice places responsibility on illustrators to manage their careers. Self-directed projects need not be, and rarely are, entirely independent, but can place an individual largely in control of managing all stages of realisation and dissemination. This will involve a whole host of necessary requirements outside of creative conception and making, such as: project management, liaising with various stakeholders, identifying and securing funding stream, ensuring publicity, outsourcing any technical support and so forth.

Illustrators are therefore required to be literate, if not accomplished across wide areas of knowledge. To sustain their career, the autonomous illustrator must be ingenious, adaptable and entrepreneurial. When not expert themselves, they must be proactive and adroit in seeking realistic and appropriate solutions.

<u>Analytical thinking</u>
Methodical and logical thinking or reasoning; the ability to identify and solve problems.

Often illustrators form supportive networks where experience and knowledge can be shared, exchanged or traded. Forums may be virtual, connecting individuals via online medias or platforms. Like-minded individuals also form collectives, sometimes sharing working environments or studio spaces where individual practices and collaborative partnerships co-function.

Can illustration ever be authorless?

It is not only authorial and autonomous practices that have introduced the illustrator as a public-facing figure. Illustrators create a sense of identity through establishing a distinctive visual aesthetic. This recognisability can establish an individual's associations with a particular field of work, i.e. advertising, editorial and interior design. Reputations for dealing with particular themes or subject matters can be reinforced, particularly when illustrators become ubiquitous and are expected to be found within certain contexts or environments. Distinguishability communicates reliability and continuity of performance to a commissioner; visibility keeps the practitioner in mind, a reminder of their professional proficiency in a highly competitive industry. However, once these associations are consecrated it can be difficult to distance oneself from those expectations.

Recognisability and visibility, whether by name or style, also bring into question whether an illustrator can ever truly be independent from the content, messages and impact of the work they deliver. An illustrator may wish to remain anonymous for various reasons: to maintain a personal distance, ensure an impartial reception, etc. However, online profiles are often very publically accessible with the intent of ensuring professional visibility. Contact details are readily available and social media platforms allow for wide-reaching commentary and opinion to be voiced.

To use the example of a commissioned pictorial image, decisions as to what and how the content is portrayed in the illustration; the emphasis of the message, the sympathies it suggests, may all be dictated by the client, art director and/or editors. That illustration, then rendered in a distinctive visual language and available to public reception, unmistakably carries the stylistic signature of the illustrator who produced it. Such a situation could find an illustrator being criticised or called to account for works in which they had restricted creative input and/or limited knowledge of the wider debates that the work sits within.

PART 2: ILLUSTRATION AND RESEARCH

Within illustration the term 'research' is used to describe many forms of investigative and interpretative practices. These methods can initially appear disparate or unrelated, for example, the following can all be described as forms of research: internet searches, reading, annotating, conducting fieldwork, creative experimenting, testing materials, interviewing, discussing ideas and so forth. This can leave the process of research elusive and encourage the common misconception of research being separate from the overall creative project. This is not so. Research is ingrained within the creative process. It is necessary when gaps in knowledge, a problem or a question is identified and further insight or experience is needed in order to progress, arrive at a solution or offer new propositions. This process is not confined to a particular point within any illustration project but rather is ongoing and actively impacts the development of the work. Some gaps in knowledge can be expected while other areas in need of development or further investigation will be unexpected and emerge as the project matures. The method or interpretative practice necessary will be governed by the nature of the concern as well as the preferences, habits and interests of the individual practitioner.

While there are so often recurring themes and ways of working within an illustration practice, the illustrator's methodology is often tailored and performed ad hoc to suit individual projects. Methods are always context specific and must be relevant to the task at hand. Familiar approaches may be tweaked or combined to create inventive multi-methods in direct response to the circumstances and situations the illustrator finds themself in.

The ensuing discoveries, interests and apprehensions that can arise as part of the research process inform and propel the project forward, sometimes in entirely unforeseen ways. These developments should not be feared, but rather expected and enjoyed.

A social practice

Illustrators have a heightened sensitivity to context. As a visual communication art form that is often applied and mediated, *context* is more readily understood as the situating and placement of the work. Illustrators are always urged to consider to whom it is that they intend to speak to and what information they intend to convey. They are innately audience and context aware; anticipating variability of reception and response, and thus tailoring their methods of interpretation accordingly. Such concerns are not limited to the latter stages of an illustration project at which point works become public facing. This receptivity and adaptability to context and audience is so deeply ingrained within the ontology of illustration, it is always at play. Ingenuity is a principal expertise of the illustrator and this is evident throughout the methods they use.

Illustration is fundamentally engaged in the social world because it is produced to perform within it. Audiences exist in real-world contexts and encounters with illustration are not limited exclusively to the traditional spaces where the arts are usually experienced. In short, illustration is inclusive, people orientated and able to operate in everyday, social life. With communication, audience and context being central leitmotifs, illustration research methods often involve direct engagement with the social world.

The illustrator's strategy might take its lead from the practices and activities of everyday life (see Chapter 3: Reporting). Rather than formal, empirical research methods, these quotidian interpretation practices are the kind used by anyone and everyone to gain insight of a social situation. In many of the methods we discuss, the illustrator emerges as a highly present figure. Rather than working covertly or at a discrete distance, they are highly involved, acting as facilitators and/or joint participants within the research encounter (see Chapter 6: Education). These methods may be considered to be the work of illustration (see Chapter 5: Activism), or emerge from the illustrative research activity (see Chapter 6: Education).

Subjectivity

The principle of being open to multiple and variable interpretations.

Research into, through and for illustration – a framework for categorising methods

Illustration research methods oscillate between a wide range of practices that encompass any combination or number of studious, practical, theoretical and creative-making activities. While we adhere that illustration methods are often multipurpose and transferable, albeit adapted to requirement, Christopher Frayling's (1993)[1] oft-cited distinctions of research *into, through* and *for* art and design is a useful model to help distinguish between categories of research practices in relation to illustration.

Within the chapter designs of this book we have not explicitly specified the methods addressed as belonging within these categories, nor do we show any preference between them. A methodology is a tailored process specific to individual needs and so often Illustration interpretive practices have simultaneous uses informing a project in a multitude of ways. Rather, we consider the framework divisions of 'into', 'through' and 'for' helpful in emphasising the breadth of what can validly be described as 'research' within illustration, and furthermore, as an aid for illustrators to better understand the roles their methods play within their individual practices.

RESEARCH *into* ILLUSTRATION Critical studies of illustrative practices. This might involve analytical discourses concerning illustrative works or artefacts; methods and processes within illustration practices; historical studies relating to illustrative movements and contexts, the works and legacy of individual practitioners or collectives and so forth. Such research may or may not be conducted by illustrators. This text can be regarded as an example of research *into* Illustration.

RESEARCH *through* ILLUSTRATION Research conducted and performed through the act of illustration practice. This might involve: creative experimentation across materials, tools and processes; development work exploring different and/or innovative ways in which illustration may be performed and/or operate; action research to test ideas or enable the development of projects, for example, peer group discussion, exhibition and/or performing of illustration. Practice-led and practice-based research falls within this category, the former describing knowledge that is acquired and develops through creative acts, and the latter whereby knowledge is contained and described within a creative work.

RESEARCH *for* ILLUSTRATION Preparatory work to inform the development of a project or to produce an outcome. This might involve sourcing reference materials for creative inspiration; acquiring technical skills or learning processes necessary to produce outcomes.

Rigour in illustration

As a public-facing communication arts discipline, illustrators must assume responsibility for the messages they impart to the world. Research journeys are seldom straightforward; they can begin with an assured intention that ends up being merely a point of departure toward an entirely unexpected project. Illustration interpretation practices are also likely to be highly inventive, impromptu and/or led in part by tacit instinct. While no two methodologies will ever be the same, it is still possible to strive for and ensure a rigorous illustration practice. Even when working intuitively it should still, albeit retrospectively, be possible to comprehend and justify the rationales for decisions made.

It is important to comprehend that difficulty, and even failure, does not always imply that a method has been unsuccessful. Some ways of working, particularly those that are new to the practitioner or even novel as research methods, will require perseverance, testing and adaption if needs be. Critical reflection and analysis are key to rigorous practice, alongside regular contemplation of motives to ensure choices are justifiable, convincing and thorough.

The following points provide an adaptable set of considerations to be referred to periodically throughout projects. It may be helpful to answer these questions in writing or through discussion with a supportive peer group. Keeping a record of responses can help chart progress and reveal areas for development.

What are the aims and intentions of your project? For clarity, aims identify areas of concern or interest, i.e. I aim to explore the housing crisis in my home town. Intentions describe what you would like to achieve through your practice, i.e. I intend to showcase experiences of homelessness from a range of different perspectives.

What are the various methods you can use to acquire the information, experience or knowledge you need to progress? (It may be helpful to refer to the previous section outlining research into, through and for illustration.)

What research methods are best suited to the needs of the project and why?

What methods do you prefer and why?

What factors might inform or influence your results?

Do these influence factors then compromise your project in any way? If so, how?

How do you determine what success and failure of methods are relevant to your aims and intentions?

How much time do you invest in pursuing a line of inquiry before moving on or adapting your methods? What governs this decision-making?

Are you documenting, storing and/or systematising your progress in such a way that it is coherent and readily available for reference as necessary?

Are you able to position your practice and/or the project against other works, illustrative or otherwise, exploring similar themes?

What audiences/participants/collaborators/facilitators will you need to engage with your work?

What are the best methods for engaging stakeholders with your project, as necessary? (It may be helpful to refer to the previous section The principles of illustration practice, describing common strategies, behaviours, tools and instruments.)

Through what forms – material, physical or otherwise – should illustrative works be realised, and why?

What are the relevant contexts for these works and how do you envisage them operating? How can this be tested?

Objectivity

Emphatic and verifiable interpretations of knowledge or information.

Originality in illustration

A contribution of 'new knowledge' that is of value to the disciplinary field and/or subject area is often a stipulation of professional research practices. While this may seem like a tall order, an offering of 'new knowledge' need not be such a daunting proposition. It might simply refer to a way of working not previously tried before, or the address of a subject matter from a unique perspective. It is also possible to reach the end of a research project, having explored a subject by all possible and appropriate means, to discover there is no new knowledge to be found; this can also be considered 'new knowledge'.

Within illustration practice, originality can encompass so much more than the all too frequent emphasis on developing a distinctive 'style' or 'visual language'. Illustration is able to contribute originality through the subject matters it addresses, the methods it uses to explore them and the knowledge that is brought to light by these creative investigations. The term 'originality' is not only used to denote universally pioneering works, it can also refer to the discipline specific achievements or the personal development of a practitioner experimenting with a new way of working. All of these endeavours require courage and risk-taking. This non-exhaustive list offers ways in which originality through illustration practice might be demonstrated:

Addressing an issue or topic underexplored by illustrators.

Collaborating with a practitioner from another discipline.

Collaborating with another illustrator at a different stage in their career.

Conducting critical inquiries of pre-existing illustrative works and/or movements never before analysed.

Engaging an audience previously unfamiliar with illustration as a discipline.

Incorporating research methods from other disciplines into an illustrative practice.

Incorporating a site-specific illustration work into a new location.

Introducing a pre-existing illustrative work to a new audience.

Making a visual interpretation of something directly observed but never before visually represented.

Placing or performing an illustrative work in an environment where illustration has never been encountered.

Producing illustrations to accompany non-literary texts not previously illustrated.

Producing a new illustrative interpretation of a pre-existing illustrative work.

Synthesising illustrative concepts or methods in new ways.

Testing the transferability of an illustrative methodology within a new research subject.

Theorising illustrative practices.

Using illustration to conduct research into a subject thus far unexplored through creative investigation.

Using illustration to visualise non-visual concepts.

Using a process or media unfamiliar to illustration practice.

Using illustration to address concerns within another discipline.

Endnote

1. Frayling, C. (1993), 'Research in art and design', *Royal College of Art Research Papers*.

<u>Qualitative research</u>
Research processes using methods, often observation, which yield subjective feedback or data. The information collected is often descriptive and not numerical.

2 AUTHORSHIP

026 — Tell me a story
  — Narrative components
029 — Narrative inquiries:
  different ways of thinking about narrative research
036 — The autoethnographic illustrator
040 — Adaption and interpretation
053 — Picture visual research
058 — Illustrative writing

THE ILLUSTRATOR-STORYTELLER
IS ENGAGED
IN A MULTI-LAYERED PROCESS.

Tell me a story

Storytelling is regarded as a central tenet of illustration practice. Regardless of the ease of affiliation, the construction and delivery of narratives is a highly skilled endeavour. The ability to convey narratives successfully, here meaning to communicate as intended while maintaining audience interest, should not be taken for granted. It requires much deliberation, planning and development, both intellectually and through creative practice.

The illustrator-storyteller is engaged in a multi-layered process. If not working with a pre-existing story, the narrative must first be authored. It must then be decided how the story will be told. What are the various nuances that will help pronounce the desired, distinctive characteristics? For example, will the story be evocative of a particular genre? Will it be biased from the perspective of a particular character? Is there an overarching message that must ultimately be understood?

Stories that are essentially the same can be told in a myriad of different ways with different effects. The introduction of a subtle detail, a shift in emphasis or a change in viewpoint can drastically influence, or even change entirely, how a narrative communicates. When narratives are illustrated, a further consideration is how this content will be described visually. Again, decisions as to what graphic approach to use, the content of the imagery, how this information will be composed and organised are far from arbitrary. These decisions are crucial in determining how readers will navigate and contemplate the information presented.

Academic theories of narrative, known collectively as narratology, provide an intellectual framework through which to understand the mechanisms in operation within specific narratives. This is a useful tool, which can help inform the illustrator-storyteller's individual practice and visual work. For example, being able to critically identify the various elements performing in an inspirational film or graphic novel will allow the precise factors determining the particular qualities of that narrative to be identified. These insights can then be used to inform the illustrator's practical work.

Narrative components

There are basic concepts within narrative theory that can be utilised by illustrators as starting points to consider how best to author and construct their visual stories. Within any narrative there are three essential layers present: the narrative text, the fabular and the story.

A *narrative text*, as defined within narrative theory, does not only apply to a linguistic manuscript or document. A narrative text refers to any medium or container through which a story is being communicated. The narrative text is the holistic delivery of a story. In this sense, a comic, a painting, an animation or even a model or diorama may be regarded as a narrative text. Illustration outcomes that intend to convey a story can be regarded as narrative texts. The form and means of delivery through which we communicate our stories actively impacts on how and what it communicates.

The *fabular* is the core information within the narrative. The fabular differs to how the story will be eventually told, and refers only to the fundamental contents of the narrative. Defining the fabular may be a useful practical task for the illustrator before beginning to plan how the narrative will be visually presented. This could be considered as an inventory of sorts, outlining details such as a list of characters, settings or locations, and a chronological time frame of the events that take place. How the fabular is then organised and visually presented will give the story its individual characteristic identity. Depending on the what the illustrator intends to make explicit, not all of the information within the fabular need necessarily be revealed.

The *story* is how the narrative will be communicated. While the fabular describes the elements of the narrative, the story may present these details in a number of different ways. This is the point at which the narrative becomes individual, a unique recounting of the fabular that gives the story a distinctive quality. The story may portray the events of the narratives in an order other than the chronological time frame of the fabular, narrative may be recounted from the perspective of a particular character, which then distorts the viewpoint. Emphasis may be given to particular events, which may either imply them as being more or less important. The story is the telling of the narrative.

EVENTS

Events refer to the happenings and situations that enable the narrative to progress and develop. The weight of importance allocated to the events will inform how the story communicates. Not all events need be imbued with equal importance; some events may be pivotal in determining the narrative situation. These are known as a dramatic climax or a crisis, and can appear at any point. Other events may be more minor but serve to progress the narrative between the more major events, and maintain the internal logic of the story.

For example, if a character suddenly appears without reason in a new location, it may need to be explained how and why they arrived in that setting before the narrative can proceed. As stated previously, the story as told may not follow the same chronology as the fabular, in which case the presentation of events also might not a follow a linear time frame. For example, take a narrative that includes what happens to a group of characters before and after a major car crash. There will be other events leading up to and then following the crash, but the car crash is the main event, which can also be described as a crisis or a dramatic climax. The car crash may occur midway through the chronological time frame of the fabular, yet the illustrator may decide to begin the story with crash and then transport the audience back and forth within time. If portraying a non-linear narrative, the illustrator will have to carefully consider sequencing and/or visual presentation to ensure the story remains coherent.

NARRATOR

Stories always have a narrator. The narrator does not refer to the illustrator, but rather to the point of narration from within the story. The narrator is the agent by which the narrative text is related to the audience. The narrator may be external and entirely removed from the events of the story. This could be considered as an outside perspective relaying how the narrative unfolds, without being involved or ever referring to their own position, much like a reporter. Conversely, the narrator may be more overtly present and self-referential. The narrator could be in the role of a character, or an agent delivering the narrative from their particular viewpoint.

FOCALISATION

Focalisation is the term used to describe the point of view through which a story is told. This may also be encompassed within the role of the narrator but

---

Metaphor

A literary device in which one thing is used to poetically describe something else with which it is not immediately associated.

Narratology

A branch of criticism rooted in structuralist thought and linguistics, narratology is the systematic study and analysis of narratives and narrative structures, and how we create, understand and are shaped by them. Narratology began with the writings of Vladimir Propp (1895–1970) and Mikhail Bakhtin (1895–1975); other key literary theorists who shaped our understanding of narrative theory include Roland Barthes (1915–1980), Algirdas Greimas (1917–1992) and Gérard Genette (1930–2018).

not always necessarily. The focaliser, more specifically, refers to how events are being perceived, i.e. through a particular character's perspective, while the narrator is more explicitly the means through which this information is communicated. The focalisation within a narrative may also be flexible, with the story being told from various viewpoints and with various opinions.

The illustrator can translate this notion of the narrator and focaliser visually and consider how it might inform graphic composition. For example, the illustrator may decide not to portray a plotline impartially, as it would be understood within the fabular, but instead may deliver this information from the perspective of a particular character. This may heavily dictate the content and presentation of the imagery, particularly if the intention is for the audience to 'see'.

ACTORS

The actors or agents within a narrative can also be understood as characters. Actors perform functionally, experiencing or causing the events within the narrative. These characters may have major or minor roles, having more or less influence within the unfolding of events as need be. Actors do not need to be human or anthropomorphic – a building or location may take on the role of a character and can thus be an actor within the story.

SEQUENCE

Sequence describes the ordering of the presentations of time and events contained within the narrative, and is intrinsically linked to how the audience perceives time. Illustrators can creatively consider how their narratives can be sequenced in order to control what information is revealed and when. Sequences may follow the same chronological time frame in which events occur within the narrative – these are described as linear narratives. Non-linear narratives might transport the viewer back and forth, disrupting the chronological time frame. This may be used tactically as a device to build tension or prompt intrigue through delaying certain plot revelations. Non-linear narratives need careful planning in order to ensure comprehension is maintained, so that interest can be sustained.

Other ways of presenting narratives may completely disregard linear, frame-by-frame, reading and instead present stories in ways more akin to maps or assemblages. In these circumstances, it may be difficult to identify more familiar narrative structures such as clear beginnings, middles and ends. This can be used strategically when wanting to avoid definite resolutions or offer stories open to multiple interpretations.

Sequences can consist of static illustrations, moving images, audio clips, objects, etc. The way that illustrators consider sequence will be informed ultimately by the mode in which they choose to deliver their narratives. For example, physical, printed pages of a publication offer different opportunities to that of the gallery space or screen-based platforms.

STORYWORLD

All narratives exist within a unique *storyworld* that describes the wider environment that the story is situated within. Even if understood as non-fictional or reminiscent of a recognisable reality, the narrative, and all the components within it – characters, locations and events – occupy a distinctive 'universe'. This universe is the conceptual setting the story inhabits. It may never be fully represented or referred to explicitly, but considering the wider storyworld, even charting it visually, can help define the logics and rationales at play with your story. Features within the storyworld may include: character backgrounds and relationships; details of the environment or geographic locations; social and political dynamics, historical time frames, etc.

Even the most surreal or fantastical narrative situation will operate with an internal logic. Having a clear understanding of the fuller storyworld can help define and justify the dynamics within an alternative reality. This awareness can also help identify what information or details need to be understood by the audience in order for them to comprehend strange and unfamiliar environments, characters or behaviours.

Incorporating details that allude to the wider storyworld may feature in a visual narrative to help support the narrative events and situations. Visual clues may be incorporated into the content of the images and the inclusion of characters who are visible but do not aid the development of the narrative; for example, homeless people within a street scene might reinforce a theme of social inequality. Even stylistic and aesthetic decisions are able to evoke a particular 'mood' or 'atmosphere' and influence the audience's understanding of the narrative environment without any explicit visual reference to a specific plot line. Using distinctive colour schemes can prompt particular resonances. For example, dark hues and tones communicate very differently to vivid fluorescent colour, and such decisions can further be informed by exploring colour theory. Similarly, the methods and processes by which images are constructed also lend meaning to narrative, regardless of what it is they graphically depict. The same visual narrative rendered fully in expressive woodcut print will communicate entirely differently than if it is created using collage. The creation of a storyworld is, for an illustrator, not only the conceptual setting for their narrative but also a visual palette through which to realise their imaginations.

Narrative inquiries: different ways of thinking about narrative research

Narrative researchers use strategies and approaches associated with storytelling to collect, contemplate, find and share meaning and knowledge about the subjects they are exploring. Within the social sciences and humanities, narrative inquiry as a process for gaining and sharing new knowledge is an established qualitative research method. There are many approaches to conducting narrative research, and methods are often creative and inventive, and shaped by the discipline within which the researchers are based. Illustrators can reflect on the uses and approaches to narrative inquiry within other disciplines and consider how they can be incorporated, and be developed, within a creative visual storytelling practice.

TELLING TALES Stories are omnipresent in everyday life and are used, often without awareness, as tools to make sense of our experiences and relationships within the environments we inhabit. Our earliest experiences of learning often utilise stories delivered in various forms; storybooks, animations, television programmes or verbal narratives shared by our guardians. We are taught to comprehend that the surreal or fantastical scenarios, such as those delivered through folktales, fairy stories, science fiction and superhero narratives, convey lessons or meanings that

---

Autoethnography

A method of inquiry, analysis and representation in which the researcher reflects on their subject matter from their personal, first-hand experience.

Paratext

A literary term describing information surrounding and framing a main text or manuscript, with the potential to influence the reader's interpretation, e.g. indexing, footnotes, appendices, etc.

AUTHORSHIP

Narrative inquiries: different ways of thinking about narrative research

relate to real world issues. As adults, we are constantly interacting and negotiating with one another through telling stories of ourselves and others. These are the means through which we can make meaning and share our perspectives of the past and the events that are unfolding around us. Because of their familiarity, stories are an accessible way to communicate to diverse audiences. Delivering information through the form of storytelling can render complex information accessible to diverse audiences. This may involve using narrative structures to organise and relate the content. The most familiar of narrative structures is the chronological ordering of beginning, middle and end. Assuming the position of a narrative researcher, illustrators can consider how visual narratives can be used to engage and communicate topics that might seem difficult to comprehend or difficult to access.

STORIES UNFOLDING

Narratives are not static, they are always in a state of development. Stories are context specific and their contents and meaning are apt to change depending on where, how and by whom they are encountered. Once a story is told, its meaning is apt to change and evolve, even if the visual signs that originally represented it are fixed, as in the example of a drawing or animation. As narratives propagate, they evolve and take on new meanings through the individual interpretations. The illustrator can only anticipate their audience's perception to a certain degree, regardless of how well-controlled the construction and delivery. Whether the narrative is a live performance, depicted with a publication or communicated orally, the audience's cognition is based on a variety of individual factors, including when and within what environment they are experienced. Different people will also interpret narratives differently according to their own interests and viewpoints, which will be informed by their own distinctive personalities, experiences and memories.

UNSTABLE REALITIES

The events of everyday life are open to multiple interpretation. Regardless of how recent or distant, once an event has occurred in history, it has the potential to be analysed, interpreted and narrated in a number of ways. Similarly, within our daily lives we occupy a number of roles that require us to present different versions of ourselves. Whether we are introducing ourselves to someone new or sharing the events of the weekend with colleagues, these are simply stories; information edited and organised to communicate to the specific audiences we are addressing.

These are not necessarily insincere but should rather be considered as alternative representations of information that invite different interpretations. The potential agendas that may be influencing how these stories are constructed, what information is presented and how, should also be considered. Contemplating this from the position of a narrative researcher can offer much insight to the situation or phenomenon being studied. Life stories, i.e. the stories we tell of our own experiences, have the potential to communicate unique perspectives. This could be applied to consider how different events, situations and experiences could be understood in different ways as a way of evoking empathy.

When conducting social research, collecting stories – for example through interviewing people, collecting oral histories or finding pre-existing accounts – is a method of research. These research findings can then be analysed to gain a wider perspective or unexpected insights. Contemplating, editing and re-organising information, events and actions into a meaningful story is a form of analysis and can be considered as a way of presenting research findings.

MAKING MEANING WITH IMAGINATION Imagination can be used as a tool to extend our understanding of areas in which we have limited knowledge. Through thinking imaginatively, we are able to contemplate human experiences or circumstances that we are aware of but have not personally endured. In this sense, fictions can be used as a method through which to have a better comprehension of a happening or situation that can never be fully known; for example, a long-past historical event. Furthermore, when in the role of narrative research, different analytical lenses can be adopted to consider the topic from different perspectives. This is a form of subjective research in which the illustrator researcher intentionally brings their own interpretation, perhaps inventing scenarios in which possible realities can be explored, allowing us to contemplate from a relatable human experience in the absence of limited historical or verifiable facts.

SUNDAY'S CHILD
Serena Katt
Published by Jonathan Cape

A group of young boys sit at a table, carefully composed and arranged, staged almost; static and rigid, frozen in time. Their clothing is carefully and meticulously rendered; the woven texture of the shirts, the neatly knotted ties, giving these figures an uncanny quality, real but not quite; characters uncomfortable in their own bodies.

These are the illustrations in *Sunday's Child*, a graphic novel and a conversation with the past; a conversation between illustrator Serena Katt and her grandfather, her Opa, the son of a Polish immigrant, who grew up in 1930s Germany. Having managed to shake off his ancestral stigma, he joined Hitler Youth like most German boys his age, and spent the rest of his school life in Nazi education. Her Opa's memories of this time – joyous, carefree and full of adventure – are recorded in a short but carefully constructed biography he penned before his death, and a collection of photographs.

Katt felt this left her with more questions than answers, her Opa's accounts at odds with everything she knew and had researched about life in Nazi Germany. In her retelling, she weaves her grandfather's story with a history she has created from her own interviews and research into the lived experience of others at that time. Katt isn't inferring judgement on the validity of these 'truths', instead she is clearly signposting the sources of the stories she is unearthing, and knitting them together through her illustrations. This is summed up neatly in the prologue to the book, 'In your words, and mine'.

This distinction is made transparent in the use of two contrasting typefaces: the voice of her grandfather and that of Katt, her story questioning, and at times, contradicting his. It is unusual for a graphic novel to have so few panels, often a single image sits panoramic across a double-page spread. With the intention to give the narrative time, the images are complex, full of detail and their relationship to the text is carefully considered. In turn, its interpretation by the reader requires time.

Image research plays an extensive role in Katt's practice. Regarding found and archival images she explains: 'I am interested in exploring and highlighting the ways in which history is recorded, suppressed, remembered and distorted through images.' For *Sunday's Child*, with its

Allegory
A storytelling device through which meaning extends beyond, or is disguised within, the presented narrative situation.

roots in a lived history, she felt it important to be rigorous with her research, emulating the period through the smallest of details: the typeface used on a shop sign or the pattern on a table cloth.

Photos were used from her grandfather's collection as well as 'filling in the gaps' with those found within online archives such as the German National Archive or the websites of World War II fanatics. At first glance, photos of Katt's grandfather tell of a contented childhood, however, Katt's own research into life in Hitler Youth tells a different story, one of brutality and oppression. Her illustrations aim to bring out the underlying unease that she sees hidden in these photos. Katt uses drawing as a metaphor for history, each redrawing (retelling) of an image moving further away from the source material and the original event.

At the forefront of Katt's process is a growing consideration for the prescribed authority given to archival images and the relationship these 'official' photographs have to those from her grandfather's collection and personal testimony. All too aware of the power structure at play, Katt questions who decides what we remember of history through images.

SUNDAY'S CHILD
Serena Katt
Published by Jonathan Cape

II

CELEBRATION
AND ENVY

2 AUTHORSHIP

Narrative inquiries: different ways of thinking about narrative research

SUNDAY'S CHILD
Serena Katt
Published by Jonathan Cape

So you are suddenly playing a central part in Germany's Wirtschaftswunder (economic miracle). You help rebuild your bank, and your country.

The autoethnographic illustrator

Autoethnography is a form of narrative delivery associated with research methodologies within the humanities and social sciences. It describes a form of narration in which the researcher-cum-narrator, is situated within the social dynamic they describe. Autoethnography draws inspiration from literary devices such as imaginative fiction, memoir, poetic reference, use of metaphor etc. and is often associated with first-person narrative delivery. Here, the narrator's 'voice' and 'point of view' is actively engaged to 'make sense'. To consider this from the position of the narrative illustration, the illustrator assumes a subjective position allowing their identity to emerge and become incorporated within the subject being discussed. The content of the narrative is open to a wide range of references informed by the distinctive identity of the illustrator, which may include literary, theoretical, observational and visual references as well as personal memory, emotion and opinion. The illustrator thus becomes a character interwoven and indivisible from the narratives they describe.

FLANAGAN'S BAR
Ruairi Fallon Mc Guigan

Roughly pebble-dashed walls, a singular hanging basket and a hand-painted pub sign reading 'FLANAGAN'S'; the Irish Pub, a familiar sight to many, except this is a simulacrum, a construction of illustrator Ruairi Fallon's imagination and physical labour.

On entering the pub, we are greeted by the trappings of the Irish global brand: symbolic references, religious iconography, surly barmen and 'in-jokes'. Framed woodcuts are the only out-of-place items, richly depicting scenes of life at Flanagan's.

Finding himself working increasing hours as a part-time barman at an Irish pub in Lewisham, South London, Fallon became acutely aware of the artificial distinction between his two lives: illustrator and barman. The *Flanagan's* project is borne from this realisation, and Fallon's intention to tell the story of the working class, Irish diaspora in London; in doing so he addresses his own position, himself an Irish native recently relocated to London.

From then on, Fallon refuses to draw a distinction between life and the project, showing the pub patrons and punters his work and asking for comment. Embedded within the community he was researching, the author and object being studied become one. This particular type of research involves being a 'native', with Fallon emotionally involved and analysis occurring through the personal. Researching academic texts on the Irish diaspora meant that Fallon learnt about the lives of others from the outside, as well from their understanding of themselves. The transgressive nature of this work meant that Fallon was party to personal and private information, meaning lines had to be drawn about what to include and exclude; his intention wasn't to create work that was confessional or sensational.

Fallon felt that in this instance, linocuts, his preferred medium, only told one side of the story, depicting the sinister, darker side of pub life: black and white, cold and detached. These were an injustice to the complexities and contradictions of the place and its inhabitants, which could be destructive and vicious while simultaneously being caring and holding an intense sense of belonging; he wasn't anonymous.

The word 'smell' is writ large in one of Fallon's many notebooks, for it was the smell of stale beer on the pub carpet, the touch of a warm pint glass, the feeling of intense adrenaline when a fight broke out or the affection and kindness afforded to him on occasion, which he wanted to represent in this work. *Flanagan's* was borne out of a desire to illustrate these emotional and sensory experiences that were so fundamental to his experiences and research. Fallon is clear that this wasn't a performance or staging, but an illustrative response to his research. He was aiming for a more direct representation of the experience; a retelling of this story through his eyes.

2 AUTHORSHIP

The auto-ethnographic illustrator

FLANAGAN'S BAR
Ruairi Fallon Mc Guigan

Photographic research images taken at Flanagan's Bar.

Lifeworld

The portrayal of a contained environment as defined by the subjective experiences of people, entities, situations and dynamics present within.

Adaption and interpretation

THE SKILL OF READING   Reading is often the principal action within any illustration project, as illustrators are often tasked with working in response to a written text. Regardless of this familiar application, the approaches to interpreting text sources vary as widely as the illustrators employing them. To read a text-based document with the express intention of illustrating it is a distinctive form of critical analysis. This is markedly different to reading for pleasure, and from other forms of academic literary analysis. When the illustrator reads, there is a particular cogitative process at play, a form of imaginative literacy; the ability to comprehend and deduce details, themes and associations that will inform a visual response. Reading is performed with the explicit understanding that interpretation will be realised visually. The illustrator reads consciously, scrutinising through a lens that filters, while also formalising creative resonances. Furthermore, illustrators assess their source material through their unique understanding of creative practice. Depending on the skill set of the individual, this may include knowledge of technical processes such as printmaking, colour mixing or graphic composition.

Often tacit but rigorous nonetheless, the strategies used will be distinctive to the individual illustrator and to the specific needs of the project. The practical actions used to navigate, identify and annotate may be highly individual and inventive, likely developed and tailored with experience.

These may include various forms of visual highlighting, marking and isolating information, even physically 'cutting', extracting and reconfiguring the content of the writing. Note-taking and annotation to aid comprehension may be highly creative, using text-based and/or pictorial languages. Regardless of approach, there will be key concerns driven by the illustrator and the intentions of the project.

The eventual outcomes will likely be informed by further research and creative experimentation but there is, within this primary act of reading, a distinctive conceptual process in operation. The various methods at play, both conceptual and practical during this preparatory work, should be recognised as integral and not precursory to the act of illustration.

Any examination will be determined by first understanding the purpose or function of the illustrations in relation to the textual content. This will be highly informed by the nature of the task, for example, the role of the illustrations may be decorative to aid comprehension of a narrative situation, or to communicate a particular tenet within the writing. The illustrative functions may also be multi-layered, for example, incorporating an aesthetic style, emphasising certain themes while also attracting a specific target audience. It is also common for an illustrator, particularly those working within a short time frame, to be considering how their illustration will be reproduced and how it will engage an audience.

The perspective of 'reading' as an illustrator can also be more pointedly utilised as a form of analytical inquiry for research purposes, i.e. to gain a distinctive interpretation that is informed by creative knowledge. In such cases the more practical, as well as theoretical, methodologies within illustration practice are also informative, for example, the understanding of materials, form, composition or craft-based making skills.

FURTHER FEMINISMS SKETCHBOOK
Lily Jones

These sketchbooks show illustrative responses to various feminist texts, including writings by Virginia Woolf and Rebecca Solnit. The practice-led analysis draws out themes and ideas that resonate with contemporary experience. These initial investigations form part of a broader project exploring everyday inequalities as described by women.

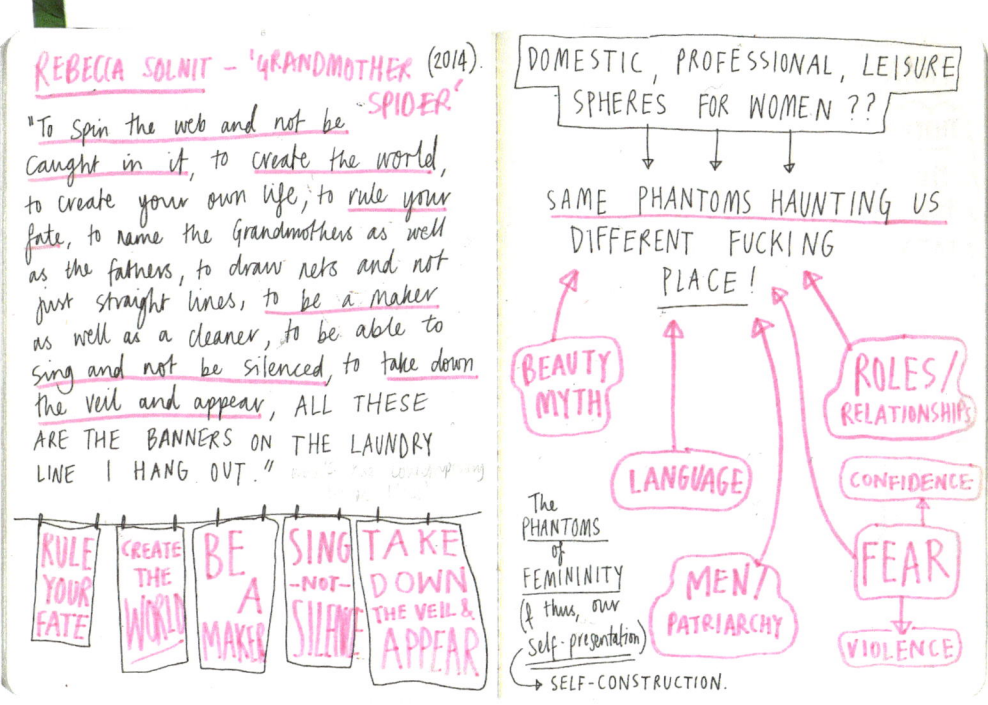

AUTHORSHIP

FURTHER FEMINISMS SKETCHBOOK
Lily Jones

Adaption and interpretation

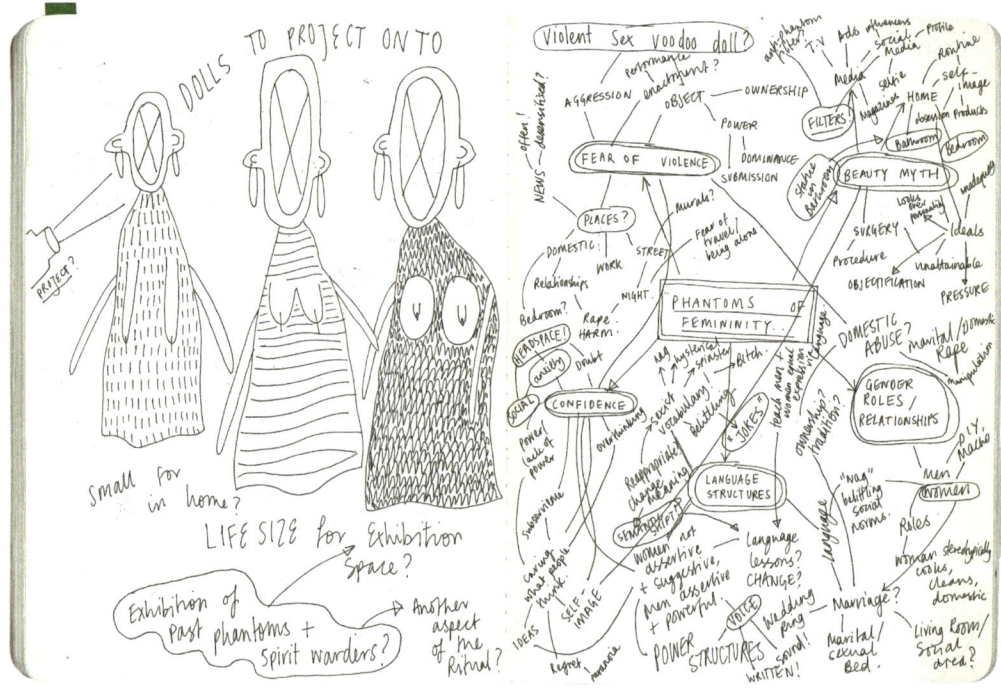

INTERPRETATIONS AND RESPONSE Considering how to interpret the information gathered and what form this response (visual or otherwise) might take is the next stage. Such interpretation begins during the reading process, in action, both in the mind and physically, in the form of visual note-taking. Reading is subjective. Meaning does not necessarily reside in the text itself, but instead meaning is brought by the reader, an idea argued by Roland Barthes in *The Death of the Author*. This infers that that there is no one reading as defined by the author, but instead there are multiple possibilities, distinct to the reader. Interpretation is individual and there is no 'correct' analysis. The illustrator brings their own world views and opinions to the text, and these colour the illustrator's interpretation and subsequent illustrative responses.

Analysing is equally about determining what to focus on as what to disregard. Information that doesn't make sense or which is misaligned with our preconceptions is ignored, while information that chimes with our judgements is read into, perhaps over-enthusiastically. The illustrator may locate themes and motifs by noticing repetition of significant objects, key phrases or ideas. Texts are full of holes, whether intentional or unintentional on the part of the author; the illustrator acts to fill in these gaps in a process of sense-making. Such content comes from the illustrator (rather than the text) and things they already know of the world.

Depending upon the conditions the illustrator is working under, this process might be directed, collaborative, or they may have full freedom. The function of these illustrations, context and audience will be suggestive of an appropriate approach. Non-exhaustive approaches may include:

Literal – depicting what has been described within the writing.

Decoration – ornamental or pattern based.

Adaption – transformation, a process of rewriting, going beyond what is a reasonable interpretation of the text.

Metaphorical – responses that depict comparative representations, which may be symbolic, analogous or allegorical.

Offering commentary or expressing opinion – depicting conceptually similar ground but offering one's own explanations, viewpoint or understanding.

Linguistic turn

Recognition of the influence of language in constructing and informing meaning.

AUTHORSHIP

Adaption and interpretation

THE PICTURE OF DORIAN GREY
BY OSCAR WILDE
Gareth Jones
Published by Four Corners Books

Four Corners – Familiars series

Published in 2007, *The Picture of Dorian Gray* was the first of what would become the Familiars series by Four Corners Books. The premise, classic texts, copyright free, are reinterpreted by artists and re-published as new illustrated editions. The design, layout, typography, as well as the physical form of the book, are considered, as well as imagery or illustrations. No two are alike, as each response is different and driven by the individual artist and their chosen title. The Four Corners Familiars series is pioneering in promoting concept-driven narrative book illustrations.

The Picture of Dorian Gray

A large, sort of squarish publication, saddle stitched with no spine making it floppy to hold, urging the reader to flip rather than turn the page, is the format taken for *The Picture of Dorian Gray*, Gareth Jones' address of Oscar Wilde's first novel. The format, along with the design and layout, is defiantly more magazine than novel, referencing the story's first incarnation as a serial, published during 1890, in *Lippincott's Monthly Magazine*.

This isn't pastiche, it is visionary and entirely apt to pull Wilde's allegory from the late nineteenth century London and render it in the visual language of the grainy 1970s news rag. The referencing is overt but so carefully realised. Wilde's unabridged text is set in columns accompanied by Gitane (the French cigarette brand) advertisements featuring beautiful young men who smoulder with a knowing sexuality.

The illustrations are black and white, granular clippings, primarily from a 1975 edition of the *Observer* magazine. They remain in context, the last paragraphs of 'SPY File' or an article on England's industrial north still running adjacent to the adverts; for their context is important, referencing the original publication format. Gitanes hang from barely parted lips; cigarettes that in this moment add to the allure but that we know will prematurely age and kill. The imagery is uncompromisingly gendered, male and homosexual. Each illustration, a portrait of a young man, either making eye contact or coyly looking away, all smoking, of course, and curiously wearing a single earring (coded message of availability within the gay community); their similarity directly encouraging closer inspection.

These images are reminiscent of illustrations used in John Berger's seminal text *Ways of Seeing*, and published in almost the same year, 1972. Berger asserts that publicity images such as these speak of the future, they are propositions that we change our lives and are concerned solely with glamour and being envied. The future in publicity images is endlessly deferred, and the more you consider how these promises of transformation will make you feel, the more you realise how far away you are from getting there. The character of Dorian Gray expresses the desire to sell his soul, and in return, a portrait ages instead of him, becoming a record of all his misdemeanors. These illustrations liken Dorian Gray's pact with his own image to the tacit agreements we make every day with publicity images.

Illustrations here don't aid visualisation of characters or settings, nor do they depict any action taking place, not directly. This is not representational but transformative. Wilde is omnipresent as the originator, but this edition was more akin to a form of re-enactment, a reimagining in which Jones' authorship was equal to that of Wilde.

A young man of extra-ordinary personal beauty

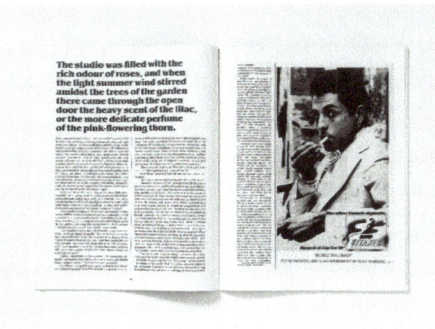

The studio was filled with the rich odour of roses, and when the light summer wind stirred amidst the trees of the garden there came through the open door the heavy scent of the lilac, or the more delicate perfume of the pink-flowering thorn.

When his servant entered, he looked at him steadfastly and wondered if he had thought of peering behind the screen. The man was quite impassive and waited for his orders. Dorian lit a cigarette and walked over to the glass and glanced into it.

All art is quite useless.

Author

A title attributed to an individual or group responsible for the production of a literary or creative work.

AUTHORSHIP

Adaption and interpretation

MEMORY PALACE
VICTORIA AND ALBERT MUSEUM
2013
Curated by Laurie Britton Newell and Ligaya Salazar

Memory Palace at The Victoria and Albert Museum is part illustration and graphic design exhibition, part spatial reading experience. An original piece of fiction, *Memory Palace*, purpose written by author Hari Kunzru, informs the content and the structure of the exhibition. Extracts from the narrative lead the visitor through the space, each accompanied by a visual interpretation from a different illustrator or designer.

The changing nature of reading and the publishing industry was the impetus for this curatorial investigation, while simultaneously attempting to tackle head-on the complexities of exhibiting works inherently uncomfortable in a gallery setting. Curators Laurie Britton Newell and Ligaya Salazar, aware that illustration and graphic design are conventionally experienced in their mediated from. When reproduced for publication and intended for viewing at close-range, engagement is intimate. Showing such works in a gallery environment risks losing this close connection with the audience. With this in mind, illustrative and graphic works were commissioned specifically for this project and are produced through design/illustrative methods with the specific understanding that they are to be experienced in the context of the exhibition. With each illustrator and designer given a separate passage or concept from the text, vastly differing approaches to conception and realisation ensued.

This exhibition is an experiment in textual analysis, with interpretation and translation central to the premise of the exhibition as well as author Hari Kunzru's narrative. Take, for example, graphic novelist Isobel Greenberg, who uses the form of the comic strip, adjacent panels telling a narrative, yet its shape is evocative of a stained glass window or altarpiece, evoking a sense of divine authority. Depicting imagined histories of the central characters, these narrative works reveal details the central character fails to remember. Text is interpreted though literal representation of fragmented scenes described within the text, interwoven and 'patched up' using Greenberg's imaginative world-building to create a coherent visual narrative.

Stephanie Posavec's images contain graphic tropes familiar to data visualisation and the language of statistics and facts, here used to interpret, not a specific passage in the text, but the time periods in which the book is set. Numbers crumble and drift to the bottom of the print; referencing the infrastructure, knowledge and information disintegrating in the fictional time known as the 'withering'. Intersecting, diagrammatic lines become pictorial devices representing weeds growing during the 'wilding' period when nature has reclaimed society.

Graphic artist Sam Winston attempts to add another layer of meaning to the text with his works, which explore how the periodic table is idolised within the novel. Winston questions what we idolise now in our materialistic society. His answer is a book, Charles Darwin's *On the Origin of Species*, a gold watch and a sim card. This is an illustration of concept, using ideas within the text in order to formulate his own critique of contemporary society.

Before exiting the exhibition, visitors are asked to leave behind one of their own memories within an interactive drawing experience created by Johnny Kelly and Nexus Studios. Each week a poster is printed capturing over 800 drawings submitted over the seven-day period. Here, Kelly creates the vehicle for the visitors to participate, the act of collective memory made tangible, and in doing so, illustrating the core message of the novel. Elsewhere, in a meta-narrative twist, illustrator Rob Hunter creates an eighteen-page graphic story that documents the process of curating the exhibition. This exhibition presents a collaborative approach to narrative making – between the curators, designers, illustrators, writer and space.

MEMORY PALACE
VICTORIA AND ALBERT MUSEUM
2013: MODERN GODS
Sam Winston

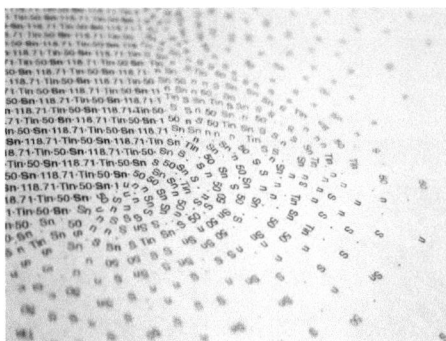

2 AUTHORSHIP

Adaption and interpretation

MEMORY PALACE
VICTORIA AND ALBERT MUSEUM
2013: MODERN GODS
Sam Winston

Research and preparatory workings for Modern Gods.

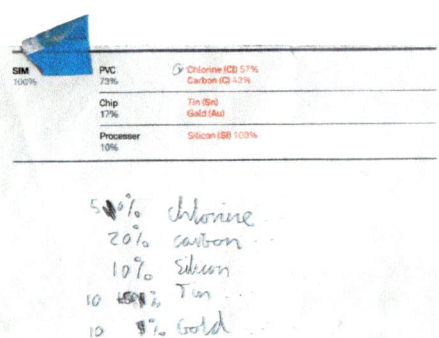

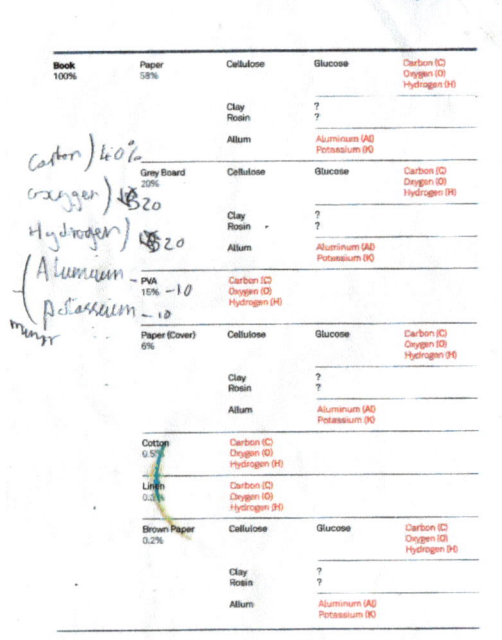

MEMORY PALACE

The third time I was brought before the Lord Inquisitor, he had on his desk the proof of my crime. It was a piece of sign, a pattern of marks joined together like a frame.

Inside the frame were intricate signs:

H	
Na	Be
K	Mg
Rd	Ca
Cs	Sr
I	Ba
Fr	Ra

44

MEMORY PALACE

It was part of something sacred and mysterious, called the Great Table of Elements. In the ancient libraries and hospitals the alphabet marks were chanted as a prayer:

/   x x   x   /
Hey-na bee!   Rod-car
/   x x   / / /
Kay-em-gee!   Shri Ba Fra!

This prayer is sounded in the language of *science* or *signs* or *signscrit*, which is the ancient language of the Lawlords from the time of the Booming. I don't know how to read the marks. I was taught how to make them, but I was never supposed to set them down. They were meant to be in my memorial, as indeed they are, sitting along a crack in the floor under my bed. I was supposed to keep them until we could use them again.

But I liked to look at them, at the landscapes of loops and lines. They made me think of hills and stormy seas and fire brimming out of molten rock. So I set them down. It was reckless; when I was taken by the wolves, they found the paper. It was trace, than which there is no greater crime. The Wilding will bring the end of trace. It will be the end of all signs separated from bodies. The bodies will just be, without sign to fly over them. All the things of the world inside themselves, dumb and silent, unnamed: that is the Wilding.

There is a slogan:

Language is a snare.

The Thing want to cut us free from the trap of words. They say we are caught and need to get away.

45

---

1. The periodic table was how ancient man mapped everything

It was composed of things called Elements — they organized them as a grid around the most powerfull

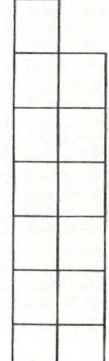

Gold

Silicon

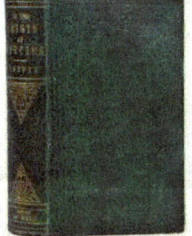

carbon

They combined Elements to make spell Objects.

49

THE BHAGAVAD GITA
Anna Bhushan
Published by The Folio Society

Illustration can function as commentary or a footnote, performing a similar role to that of marginalia or notation, providing the reader with critique, comments or illuminations, a function explored by illustrator Anna Bhushan in her illustrations for the 700-verse Sanskrit scripture, *The Bhagavad Gita*. Such instances are suggestive of the illustrator working individually rather than collectively with the author and are sometimes considered a subversive act (consider illicit annotations in university library books). Such illustrations may also provide new and inventive methods for understanding otherwise dense or complex texts. Bhushan's illustrations present how this method may be particularly applicable to complicated texts, or texts with historical interpretations or multiple philosophical or linguistic translations.

AUTHORSHIP

Adaption and interpretation

THE BHAGAVAD GITA
Anna Bhushan
Published by The Folio Society

Picture visual research

Image research is a methodology that is individual to every illustrator and yet there are common techniques that ensure this process is rigorous and varied. Researching visually usually means sourcing images for reference or photographing your own with the aim to give a more accurate or meaningful representation of time or place. Understanding how work is going to be read is key to this process, and acknowledges readers who are capable of deciphering visual signs and clues in order to add believability, richness or authenticity. Simply rendered, items such as a chair, a shoe, or a window can add so much depth to an image if it is carefully considered and researched, being suggestive of period, location, status, taste, wealth, etc.

Selecting appropriate locations in which to source these images is the first step. Archives, artists or designers (specifically those active during the period the text is set), photography (reportage photographers, personal photography collections, postcards), film, diagrams or maps, even contacting experts in the field (e.g. architect, hobbyist/enthusiast, local historian), can provide original source material.

This doesn't mean to suggest that illustrations must be passively faithful to the situation of the text. Considering the relationship between visual accuracy and interpretation is significant. The illustrator can construct new and imaginative worlds – taking references from multiples sources, times and locations as well as their own imagination. This is particularly relevant if the text is set in the future or in a completely fictitious location.

Semiotics

Rooted in linguistics, semiotics is a method for modelling the relationship between words and images, and for understanding how meaning is constructed. It can be used as a toolkit for understanding how visual communication works and the interpretation of signs. Charles Sanders Peirce (1839–1914) and Ferdinand de Saussure (1857–1913) founded the study of semiotics.

AUTHORSHIP

Picture visual research

HEART OF DARKNESS
BY JOSEPH CONRAD
Catherine Anyango Grünewald
Published by Self Made Hero

Catherine Anyango Grünewald revises Joesph Conrad's *Heart of Darkness* as a comprehensive graphic novel. Anyango's sketchbooks show the varied reference materials and in-depth research, preparation and tests conducted to create the atmospheric depiction of the classic novella.

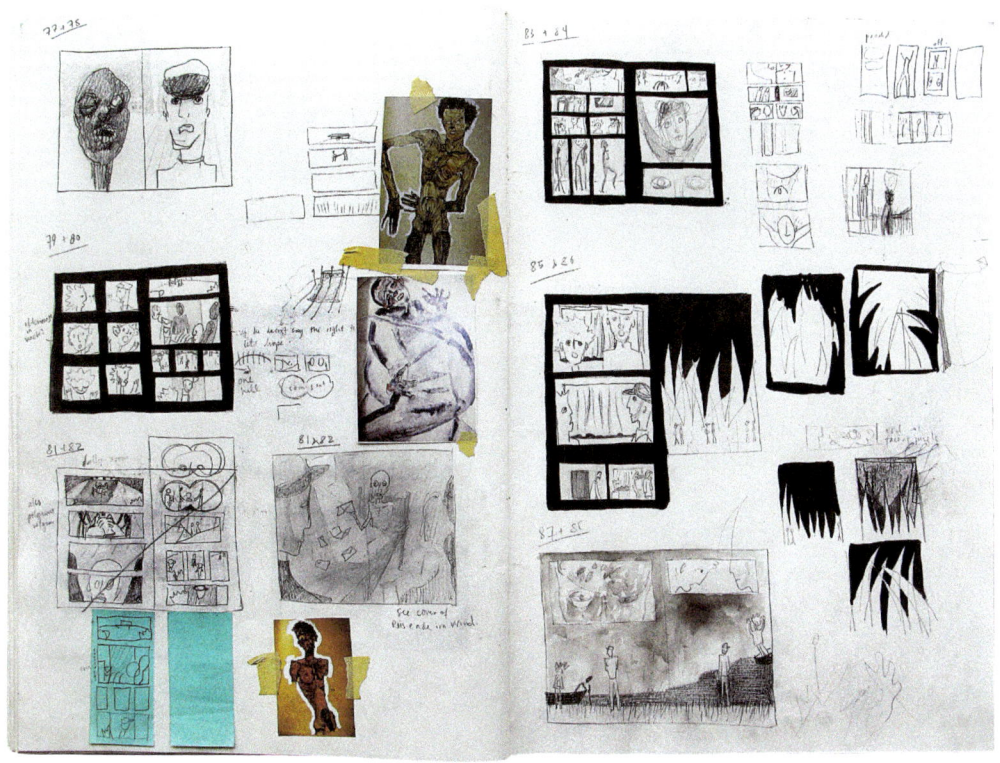

2 AUTHORSHIP

**HEART OF DARKNESS
BY JOSEPH CONRAD**
Catherine Anyango Grünewald
Published by Self Made Hero

Picture visual research

Illustrative writing

Illustrators authoring written content is a natural progression, considering the symbiotic relationship between the illustrative image and the written word. Here, illustrative writing does not refer to typographic forms presented as imagery but rather to the use of writing as an illustrative device. Illustrators often produce written material as part of a wider project to be accompanied by pictorial images such as in the case of graphic novels or illustrated narratives. Writing is often used as a method of inquiry and an analytical tool during the research process, to document investigations, findings and chains of associations. Illustrators might also consider how writing can be used creatively as an independent illustrative form and how written or spoken language might be used as a technology to extend the remits of illustrative representations.

When illustrators write they do so with illustrative intent. The strategies and behaviours that underpin illustration as a discipline are applied to writing as they would be to any other communicative form (see 'The principles of illustration practice', p. 16). As illustrators are so often called upon to visually interpret written sources when they author their own material, the same critical analysis is still in operation. Illustrators write from the vantage point of being able to inform a visual imagining in the reader's mind. While the material outcome is not in the most direct sense visual, the treatments of content, structure and delivery perform as they would in an illustrative image. Evocative descriptive language strives to bring to mind vivid scenarios, which will be uniquely envisioned by each and every reader. Creative wordplay is used in the same way that visual elements are composed to produce narratives through evocative association. Illustrative writing, like all forms of illustration, does not merely describe or translate information, it performs with affect.

BLANK SLASH
Phoebe Nightingale

A book cover bound in red book cloth opens unconventionally from a diagonal laceration, with spines on both left and right to expose the clinical white of the book stock inside. The cover eschews tradition and contains no words or images. Inside, only carefully placed typography faintly appears, devoid of punctuation it quietly asserts what is a tragic and terrifying narrative.

Phoebe Nightingale writes and designs books in which the text, design, physicality and tactility of the book are the illustrative devices integral to the 'reading'. *Blank Slash* is a nightmarish 'post truth' dystopian tale where scars appear on those who lie, and a 'skin screener' is tasked with the bureaucratic job of counting scars in order to quantify the fallibility of human nature. The text itself becomes an illustration, text left-aligned is the truth and text right-aligned is a lie. The reader is encouraged to read down the centre, the spine itself acting like a cleaver, reminiscent of the concrete poets where the typographical arrangement conveys as much meaning as the language in the text itself.

The reader is forced to become complicit and act out the story, the opening of the book akin to reopening a wound. Here, the design and materiality of the book illustrate the visual metaphor at the centre of the narrative: the scars of those who lie.

i fill in her chart while i count
i start with her name height weight age

aged 29
she gives her answer in careful stilted truth

she gives her answer in a dripping fluid lie
a fresh / oozes deceit

so i add another / to my total

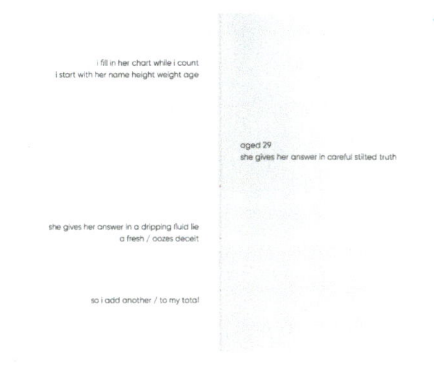

Death of the Author

An essay by literary theorist Roland Barthes (1915–1980) arguing that to assign an author to a text affects and limits the interpretation of the content.

3 REPORTING

062 — Illustrator as reporter
    — This is research
064 — How to
067 — Drawing from life
072 — Sketchbooks
    — Listening
076 — Observation
081 — A multisensory lifeworld
084 — Walking
092 — Me, you and everyone else
097 — Is this real?
    — Reporting the news

AT THE BEGINNING
OF THE RESEARCH JOURNEY,
WHAT IS ANTICIPATED COULD
TURN OUT TO BE
VERY DIFFERENT
FROM WHAT IS ACTUALLY DISCOVERED.

Illustrator as reporter

The use of illustration to document sociocultural narratives is firmly established in both historical and contemporary practices. Works concerned broadly with depicting current affairs, people and places are often described using largely generic terminologies such as *reportage, documentary* and *visual journalism*. These terms have come to describe myriad different illustrative works and practices, grouped together because of a shared concern with site-specific studies and/or an interest in describing the human experience. Casual use of these categorisations fails to acknowledge the highly complex, innovative and distinctive interpretation practices used by illustrators when responding to real world events. While adhering to more recognised conventions, the central concerns with people, social dynamics and environments, the use of the title 'reporter' as used here describes a varied set of methods that do not necessarily favour the ocular sense. For example, fieldwork practices often place emphasis on observational image making but also include *walking and/or listening* as illustration interpretative practices.

Illustrative works made in response to live events need not always be made in real time during the happening of the occasion they describe. Instead, methods might be used in combination to provide a more holistic understanding of the current affair, such as direct engagement during location visiting, supported by historical or archival research.

Any illustration project addressing a community group or a populated location as a subject matter of interest will require much logistical organisation, willingness to compromise and an emphatic approach. When on location, illustrators can seldom work entirely covertly, and it won't always be appropriate, so they must consider how to negotiate the impact of their presence on the environment and situations they describe. An ethical practice must be maintained at all times (see Appendix). However, this should not be considered an obstacle or hindrance but rather as an assurance of rigour and good practice.

Furthermore, illustrators can never be truly impartial or objective; even in the absence of an obvious human narrative, the living, breathing illustrator is always the conduit through which the understanding of their subject is described. While the illustrator, assuming the role of reporter, is engaged in a non-fictional subject, 'truths' are subjective and multiple. Rather than claiming to represent reality, illustration's strength lies in the ability to document outer and inner worlds, multiple perspectives and the immediately visible as well as the unseen.

This is research

The real world is messy and unpredictable. No matter how carefully planned a project may be, it is wise to expect the unexpected; people change their minds, circumstances change, access previously granted may suddenly be denied. Being adaptable to change, seeking out solutions and liaising with others is as integral within the illustration research process as creative making.

Preparation can be time intensive, so it is vital to make contact and establish lines of communication as early as possible. Anticipate that organisations and individuals may be unfamiliar with illustration practice or perhaps have not been involved in a creative project before. It will be helpful to prepare a clear and concise statement describing your project idea and intentions, which can easily be shared. It is important to have the consent of those you would like to include in your project. However, if this is not granted by the most direct source the project needn't be entirely scrapped. Think broadly about the different ways you could gain knowledge about the subject area of interest; are there other groups or individuals with different perspectives you could reach out to? Examples are social clubs, local councillors, community groups and religious institutions. While you may start with a clearly defined subject – what is interesting and feasible may turn out to be something completely different.

No culture can be separated from the geopolitical, economic structures and dynamics that exist globally. These forces should be seen as existing within cultures and forming links between people, cultures and locations. If making work about a community or environment outside of your own personal experience, identify who your cultural gatekeepers could be. A gatekeeper is an individual who can offer specialist insight and information, most likely because they are members of the community of interest, which might seem elusive from an outside perspective. A gatekeeper might also be able to facilitate introductions or negotiate on your behalf to develop trust between parties.

The distinction between a socially active and engaged person and 'conducting research' can be blurry – you may have already 'started researching' without even knowing it. Share your research ideas and talk about your projects, you may find that a conversation in passing reveals a useful lead. You may also already have an existing network of valuable connections. People are always engaged in multiple communities and social groups; perhaps your family, friends, colleagues, neighbours, etc, might know of someone who may be of use to your project.

A seemingly precise subject matter may be initially identified. Then, during the process of information gathering, phone conversations, email exchanges, multiple site visits etc, this original subject begins to broaden or even transform completely. This is to be expected and a breadth of knowledge will enrich your understanding of your subject matter. However, it is important to know that no single project will ever be able to describe all facets or offer all perspectives on any phenomenon.

Defining clear boundaries of what the project is and isn't concerned with will help focus and contain your research, and will help identify the information that is and isn't relevant despite how interesting it may be. Remember, no research is ever conducted in vain; a narrative or piece of information not quite appropriate now can grow into another independent project later on.

At the beginning of the research journey, what is anticipated could turn out to be very different from what is actually discovered. Strive to be flexible and creative in your approach. Adapt to the inevitable surprises and uncertainties that will occur. Know that there is always the potential for rejection when asking for help and support, particularly when others act outside of their normal remit.

Don't be dissuaded. Find doors to open. These disappointments should be seen as opportunities to try a different approach. The research process has started, and while creative making or visual responses may not have yet begun, these stages are an important part of the illustration research process.

Anthropology

A discipline addressing all aspects of human life and culture with concerns as diverse and wide-ranging as religion, belief, gender relations, material culture, world views, domestic and family structures.

How to

Establishing a clear outline of what the purpose of your research is, what subjects you intend to explore and why, will help determine what information or knowledge you require and the best ways to acquire it. This might include various strategies. For example:

— Conducting fieldwork that will require being in direct contact with the culture, communities or physical landscape being researched. By observing, describing and/or depicting peoples' behaviours and interactions within their everyday settings, the researcher can discover what is happening in the here and now.

— Archives, museums, collections or databases of knowledge can offer original, unique or unpublished historical documents and artefacts. Such publicly available documents allow the researcher to extract evidence first hand in order to form a picture from fragments of information.

— Seeking out existing investigations that address relatable issues helps establish what is already known about your subject area. Conducting practice-based research may include other creative responses and methodologies.

To research is to go in search of unknown information; it is expected that a project might begin with just an interest rather than firmly established knowledge. The subject matter might be entirely new – this shouldn't be considered a problem. As long as an entry point can be established as a first step toward gaining further insight, a research plan can be developed.

DON'T BELIEVE THE PAPERS
Mireille Fauchon

In 1912, the Croydon suffragette Katie Gliddon was imprisoned for two months in Holloway, London for taking part in the mass glass smashing campaign. While detained, she kept a diary hidden in the margins of an anthology of poetry by Percy Bysshe Shelley. Post-release, she continuously edited and revised her account with the intention of her record eventually being published. It never was.

Mireille Fauchon interprets and creatively responds to Gliddon's evolving narrative in a body of work entitled *Don't Believe the Papers*. The project forms part of a practice-based PhD that examines how narrative illustration can be utilised to describe and communicate location-specific sociocultural narratives. During this research, Fauchon has implemented various approaches and strategies, including: interpreting Gliddon's writing and poetry by Shelley, archival research conducted at The Bishopsgate Institute and the Museum of Croydon, and collecting experiences of contemporary Croydon. Through this holistic reading, Fauchon investigates how and why personal and local histories are preserved, what is deemed worthy of documentation, and how this knowledge is maintained formally and informally within the locations of experience.

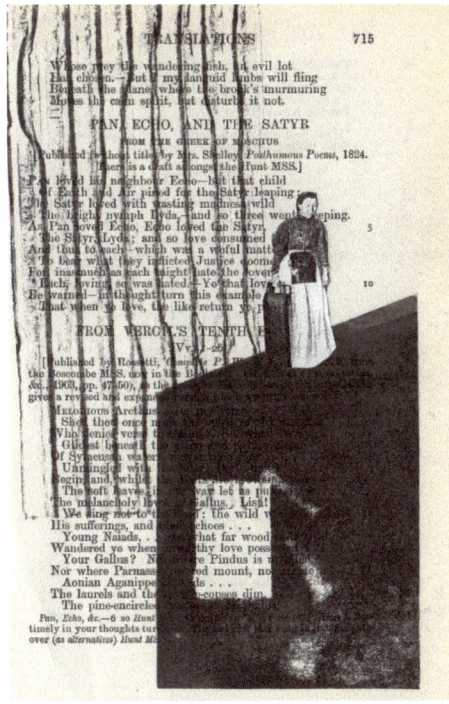
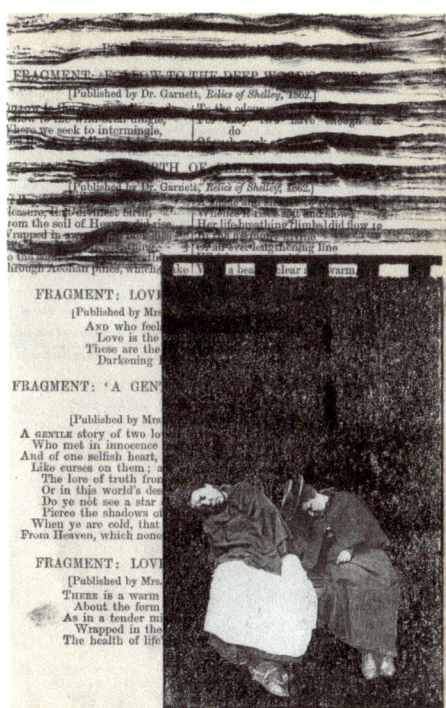

DON'T BELIEVE THE PAPERS
Mireille Fauchon

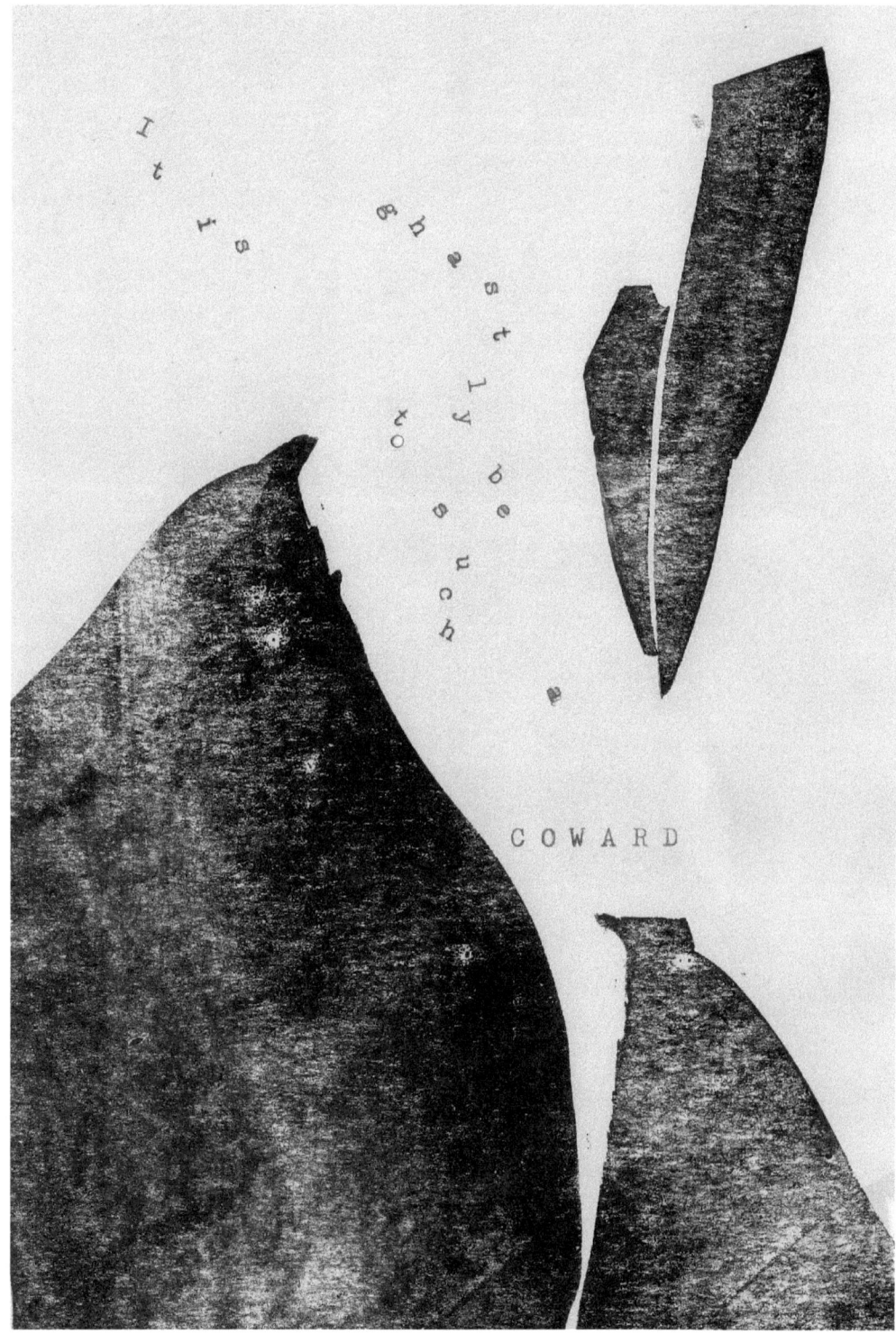

Drawing from life

Drawing from observation is a method familiar within reportage practices and is also a way of working that all illustrators are likely to use at some point in their careers. Image making is produced in real time while in situ. The illustrator is based on location within the environment of interest to record with drawing what is visible to their gaze, be it mundane or momentous. Drawing is at once an image-making tool, a sense-making technique and an outcome that can then be shared with others. Working from direct observation is not simply representation 'as seen'; it requires ad hoc decision-making as to what to select or omit from a composition. These choices are subjective and are revealing of the practitioner's personal interpretation of the environment described. Working from direct observation can convey an immediacy; a sense of being 'in the moment', which is difficult to replicate when attempted in retrospect. The materials used to create the drawings can also influence the meanings conveyed by the imagery. Different tools yield different marks, which can emphasise a particular mood or ambient atmosphere. It is also necessary to select drawing instruments and equipment that is suited to the location you will be working in. Drawing on location is commonly associated with mark-making materials such as charcoal, pencils etc, but any image-making tools or approaches, as appropriate, can be used.

CHANDIGARH –
CONCRETE AND SHADOWS
Rachel Gannon

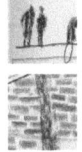

Illustrator Rachel Gannon visited Chandigarh, India's only planned modernist city, with the intention to document one of the world's most ambitious urban experiments. Designed by Le Corbusier in 1950, Gannon was interested in how Corbusier's exacting modernist ideals had been adapted to suit the lives of those inhabiting this city. These drawings made on-site, depict the relationships between daily life and the architecture of the city. Entering Chandigarh is a paradoxical experience, a mix of spatially overwhelming reality and an Indian city in the potential mode; as if Modernism has been literally dragged onto the broad plains of northern India. Gannon was keen to capture how this city feels to her; at once uncannily familiar and yet entirely foreign. It is in the truest sense a liminal urban landscape. Information is edited in the drawings, the architecture appears to dominate the frame, with shadowy figures dwarfed by the scale of the concrete structures.

CHANDIGARH –
CONCRETE AND SHADOWS
Rachel Gannon

Ethnography

People-focused research, often utilising qualitative methods such as participant observation, interviews, focus groups and creative documentary methods in order to understand the lived experiences of others.

CHANDIGARH – CONCRETE AND SHADOWS
Rachel Gannon

Sketchbooks

Sketchbook practice as a way of collating information is a research methodology in its own right. The sketchbook can be used and adapted to suit particular case studies, locations or subject matter. Illustrators will develop individual and personal ways of using their sketchbooks on location. Acting as a container for thoughts, observations and memories, the sketchbook provides a physical space to bring together found objects, studies, collected research and reference. Texture and tactility can be recorded through collecting objects.

Multiple methods can sit alongside one another, with the researcher selecting the most appropriate method to record or document a specific situation. The blank page does not prescribe a certain 'right' usage, the sketchbook promotes a personal or inventive approach. Written notes can document conversations and visual details that cannot be captured in any other way.

The format of the sketchbook, a codex, sheets of paper permanently bound into a spine, means that its contents are chronological and show events unfolding over time. Research is ordered and collated. A transportable method of documenting and collecting research, the sketchbook can be easily carried. Alternatively, an illustrator may prefer to work on loose sheets of materials in order to allow for unintended connections to be made from reordering.

Often diary-like, the sketchbook affords a private space for thoughts, reflections and personal interpretation. Although the format encourages a linear recording, it allows emerging themes and interests to be revealed by observing patterns within the research. The sketchbook actively encourages an experimental approach to research, providing a safe space for testing out new or innovative ways of recording.

Listening

The practice of listening occurs in any method where a dialogue or conversation is interpreted. There are many practices that involve speaking and listening in order to gain information or understanding.

The decisions as to how to conduct or facilitate spoken dialogues is dependent on the nature of the information required. For example, if trying to gain information about a specific topic from a knowing expert, a formally structured interview with directly pointed questions may be best suited to the task. However, a more 'naturally occurring' framework might be more suitable to allow for a looser conversation where digressions can occur.

Group discussions can encourage dialogues between people who converse through responding to one another. This can be a strategy to gain insight from within social groups or communities where the relationships, dynamics and shared knowledge are as useful as the content of the conversation.

Collecting oral histories whereby people recount their lived experiences can be particularly useful for gaining person-specific subjective insights into a particular subject, event, location or experience. Interviews, conversations, discussion groups and oral histories, can be recorded, with permission, for transcribing and later contemplation. However, practices of listening may be necessary in unexpected, ad hoc situations, whereby you find yourself speaking to someone during a chance encounter, or overhearing conversations. And while it may not always be appropriate or even possible to record, being able to *listen* is the method that can always be called to task. Listening is more than hearing the spoken words; intonation, pauses, pronunciation and use of language can also reveal many insights, for example, cultural background, influences, age, political inclinations, specialist knowledge, etc. Similarly, body language, the ease or ill-ease displayed can also offer information not revealed with words.

Indeed, the words spoken may not actually bear any relation to the meaning that will be eventually interpreted by the illustrator. The words people use to express their knowledge or experiences, particularly around sensitive subjects (not necessarily traumatic) may be carefully chosen. People speak and share narratives with an array of agendas – to protect, to exaggerate, to humble, to soothe, etc – this should be taken into consideration.

Listening is far from being a passive act; the skill lies in engaging with the information being recounted to you. While it is often necessary to interact and reply, the emphasis is on allowing another to express themselves fully, and understanding the various possible meanings and implications.

Recounting an experience is a reflective act; it requires editing, organising and articulating information. Any telling will include excluded information, disrupted chronologies and a sense of time regarding what and where things took place. The details may be edited for various reasons; deliberately for ease of explanation, to save time, to highlight significance and also simply due to what is remembered and forgotten. This all has an impact on interpretation for both the researcher who listens and the participant who tells. The intention should not be to find absolute truths but rather to understand another's perspective.

When interviewing or facilitating conversations, it is important to be mindful of power balances. Leading questions can influence an answer suited to the researcher's inquiry. The tone of the interviewer can communicate as being in authority with the interviewee as the vulnerable or submissive party. These hierarchies can be negotiated through careful planning. Being mindful of space and where interviews take place can have great impact on an interview situation, for example, a neutral space not specific to the interviewer or interviewee(s); a public space where other people are present at a distance; a location familiar to the interviewee(s); being situated among your panel or at a distance; positions of chairs, etc, will all have an influence.

Processes of recording may be visual as well as aural with words and images being used to document and record a conversation. This can occur in real time with illustrations produced in response to an unfurling dialogue. Such methods serve to simultaneously collect, edit, interpret and represent the research findings. Facilitating formal conversations and interviews for research purposes requires much preparation and foreplanning. Speaking in person, even in very relaxed and friendly environments, is a very confrontational situation. It requires establishing trust, which takes time. If this method of research is anticipated, time must be allowed to make contact with parties of interest, establishing access, ensuring intentions are understood, and permissions must be gained with clarity as to how this information will be used and stored. This can be a highly rewarding process, not only in terms of enriching projects, but also for personal development.

LANDLESSNESS
Marianne Keating

Landlessness addresses the partial and fragmented recorded history of Irish indentured labourers migrating to Jamaica. The two-channel video piece show parallel films of land and seascapes shot on location in both Ireland and Jamaica. The imagery is overlaid and intersected with texts drawn from records held by the national archives in Ireland, Jamaica and England.

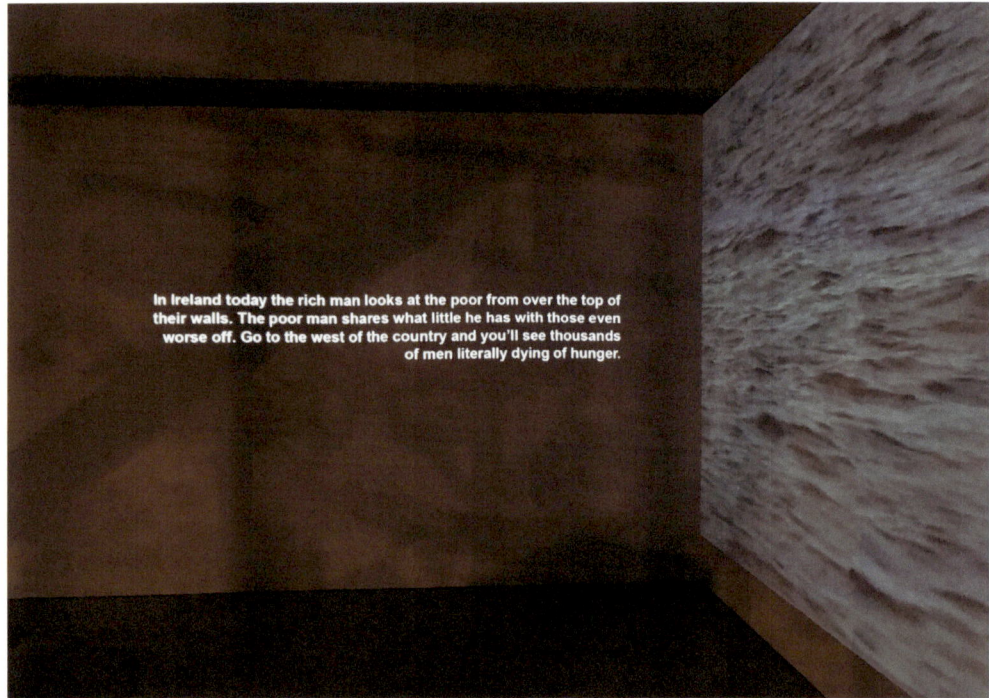

LANDLESSNESS
Marianne Keating

Observation

Observation is a well-defined research method and one used often within illustration as well as other creative disciplines and social sciences. For illustrators, drawing from observation is considered a fundamental method for learning how to represent formalities such as form and tone. Familiar exercises, such as life or location drawing, are used not only to teach the fundamentals of painting or drawing, but also to learn to look. Observation can also be used as a research method when wanting to understand a specific group of people, community, viewpoint, profession, location or activity.

Observation methods can loosely be divided into two categories, and you may need to decide which is more appropriate for the subject matter: active involvement or the detached observer.

If you decided to announce your presence by actively involving yourself in the situation you are observing, you may gain a more empathetic understanding. Your observations will be made through being engaged in activities or participating in social or cultural events. By becoming part of the group you are researching, you may be privy to information or insights that you would not normally have access to. Considerations such as how much detail you divulge about your project to the participants, or how you will behave when you are acting as a 'researcher' in a situation that is out of your comfort zone, or how you will communicate private or personal information are just some of the ethical considerations you may be faced with. Being a detached observer involves intentionally removing yourself from the situation being observed with the aim to cause as little impact as possible and to maintain an objective stance. Whether this is ever actually possible is acutely contested. Being in the situation, however detached, can change the dynamics of the situation and therefore what you are observing. People may act very differently if they think they are being drawn or photographed.

You may need to consider how you record situations, as overt documentation like note-taking, drawing or photographing is not always suitable, legal or appropriate, and you may have to rely on your memory and record information after the event. Knowing what is appropriate for the situation you are in will mean considering religious or cultural norms, as well as the legal rights of people around you. What is legal may not always be appropriate; questioning what participants might find invasive or uncomfortable is a good place to start. Each situation is different and will hold different challenges. Therefore, planning, as well as being actively aware of these ethical issues, is necessary.

LIEU DE VIE
Marguerite Carnec

French-born illustrator Marguerite Carnec's documentary project *'Lieu de Vie' (Living Place)* focuses on the demolition of the *Jungle*, a refugee camp on the outskirts of Calais, France, in 2016. These illustrations are alternatives to the news images that accompanied many of the stories about migration. The illustrations are showing us something different. Dissatisfied with the very western-centric news coverage of *The Jungle*, Carnec set about recording her own experiences of volunteering at the camp.

'My aim was to give an alternative representation to the media's biased black-and-white coverage of the Jungle that often dehumanised refugees. It illustrates my personal experience of meeting those that lived there, witnessing their everyday struggles, the injustice of their situation and the hardships they faced whilst waiting for asylum.' Marguite Carnec, AOI World Illustration Awards.

This is what we can call the 'humanising effect' of illustration. Carnec owes much to a legacy of illustrators like Sue Coe, whose work so sharply and painfully reports on the meat industry and animal exploitation, as well as many other highly political and divisive issues. Like Coe, Carnec's work aims to look past the so called 'cause' and the rhetoric, 'the plight of the refugees', in this case, and instead address the human. Uncomfortable with the power relationships inherent in much of this type of research, Carnec decided to put her initial intentions aside and volunteered to work in the camp instead. Once there, it felt more authentic to draw what she saw rather than comment on the wider political agenda. Drawing in situ offers a different power relationship. Conspicuously on show, the illustrator cannot hide behind a camera, and the drawings produced are instantly visible.

The final images, a set of large-scale mono prints, are an imaginative retelling of events. A personal interpretation by the illustrator can create a record of events that can engage wide audiences through capturing the singularities or details that make accounts more 'real' and thus accessible. Carnec does this by highlighting the Nike 'swoosh' on a trainer or the iPhone being used to take selfies. These details also attest to the illustrator having witnessed the events first-hand. Illustrators like Carnec recognise the importance of making images that an audience can identify with and understand. Illustration has the ability to engage with those peoples and places being documented through its process, and with an audience through its output.

LIEU DE VIE
Marguerite Carnec

LIEU DE VIE
Marguerite Carnec

A multisensory lifeworld

The world is alive and animated, and our comprehension of it is informed by all of our active senses. While Illustration is arguably fundamentally concerned with the production of images, what inspires us is informed beyond what is immediately visible. There are diverse ways of understanding a situation or experience; smells, sounds, touch, emotion and instinct all inform our reading.

As researchers, we respond to our investigations as humans, not machines or image-capturing devices. We make meaning through multisensory engagement, and the visual is no more valid than other senses. Working in documentary mode needn't only be limited to visual depictions of what has literally been seen, and in some circumstances this may be actively inappropriate. It may be a faithful translation of what was experienced, but this doesn't make it more 'authentic'.

A vivid visual recording is not always sufficient to capture the vivacity and dynamics resonating within the lifeworld we attempt to portray. When conducting research – be it a site visit, working in an archive or engaging with participants – being attuned to feelings is a methodology. Being receptive to smells, sounds and touch and actively trying to comprehend how they inform experience can then influence visual response in order to evoke the desired understanding in the viewer. Furthermore, it may be pertinent to consider whether expressions of illustration must extend to stimulate audiences in ways other than visual.

LAYERED TIME
Emma Harry

 Details of microscopic views of rock are rendered in chalk collected from the Deal to Dover coastline. Emma Harry's practice explores how time is understood and recorded within the interplay of elements and their effects upon the landscape.

<u>Anthropocene</u>

A proposed epoch referring to the current geologic age in which human action has been dominant in influencing the development of the Earth's natural environment.

LAYERED TIME
Emma Harry

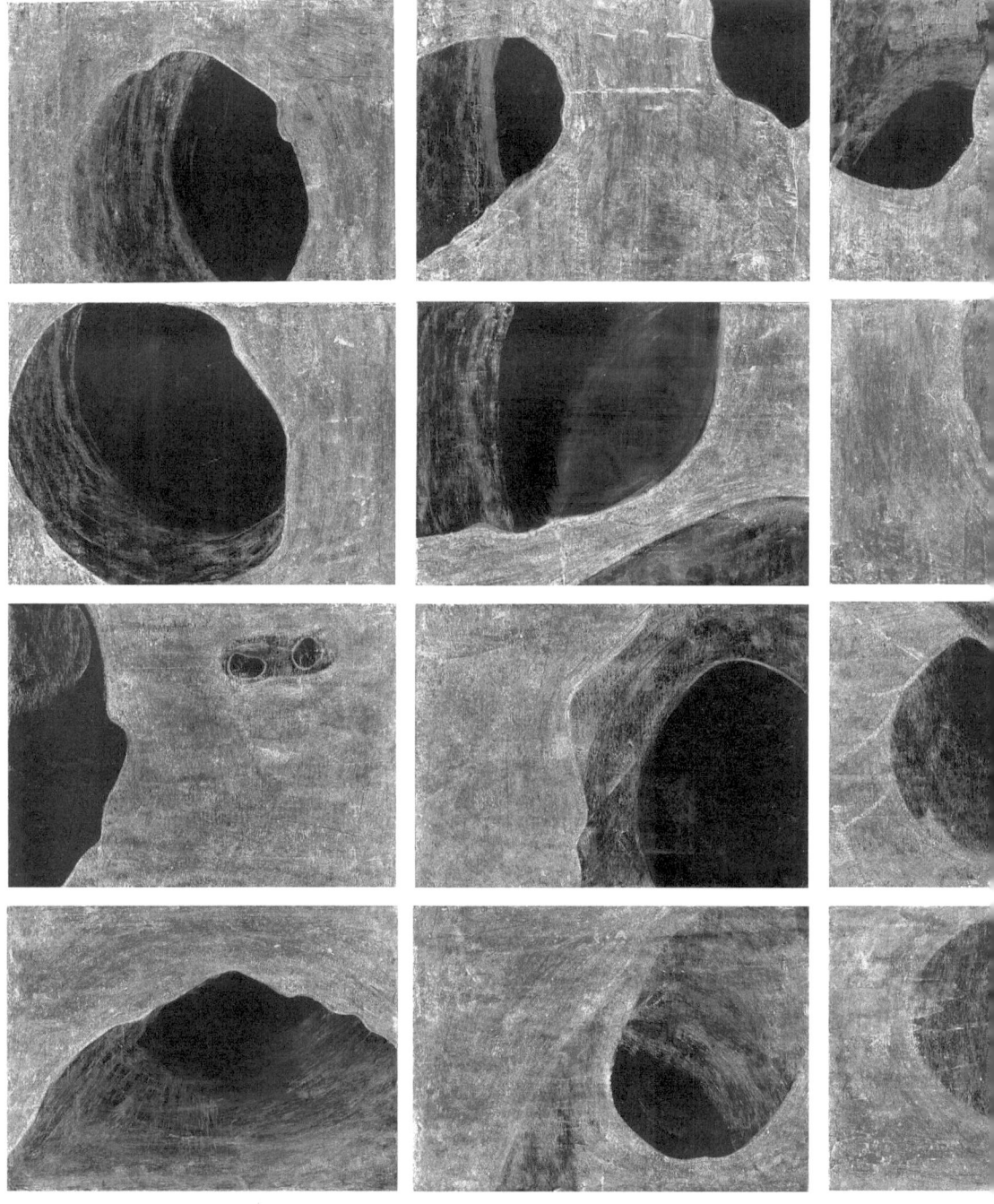

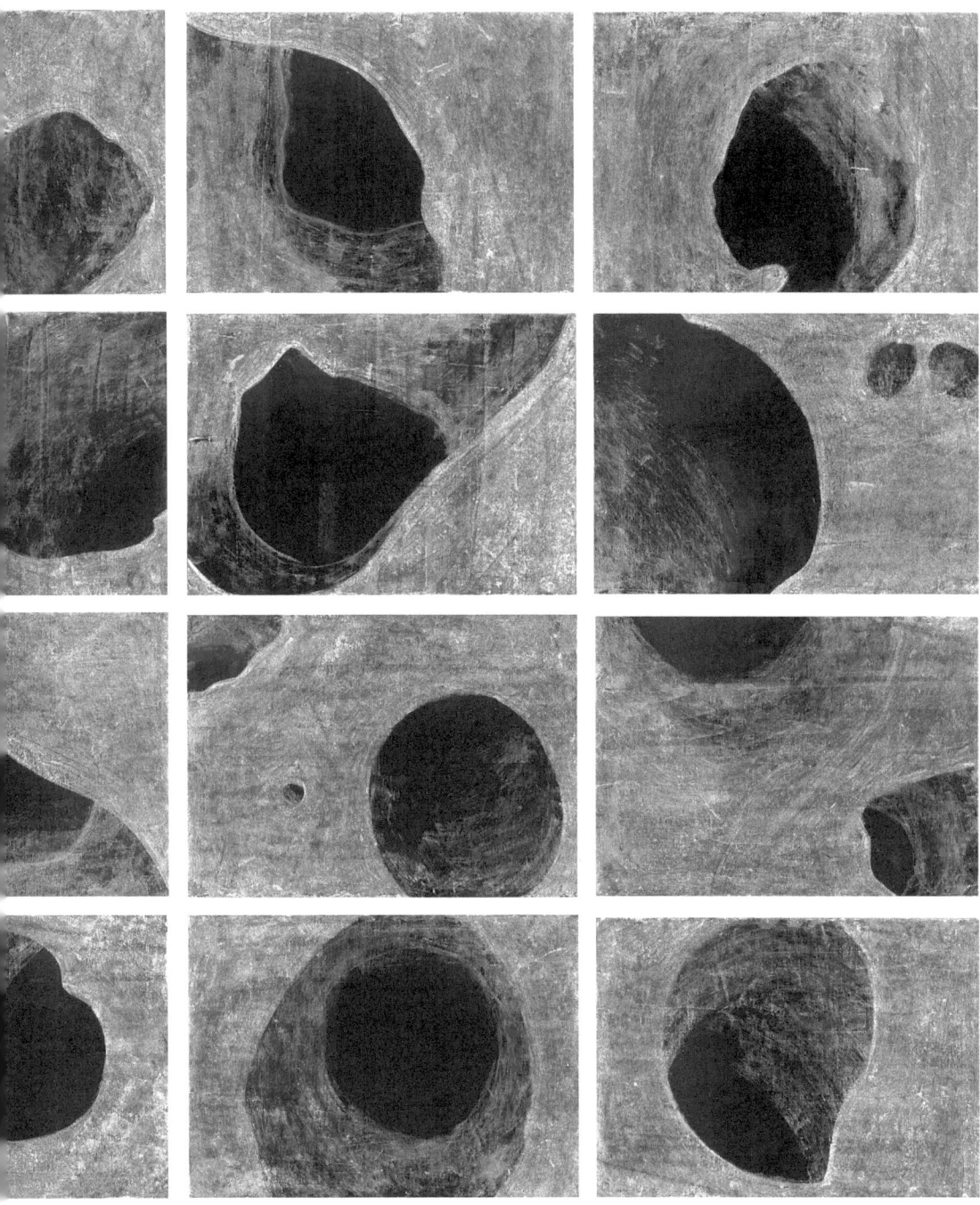

Walking

Sitting between psychology and geography, psychogeography is a method for critically engaging with the urban environment through playful or experimental means and always on foot. Play needs rules, and often a set of invented restrictions or guidelines are put in place in order to navigate a space. Taken up more recently by illustrators, it has been used to explore and examine specifically urban issues such as gentrification or the privatisation of public space. It is about being awake to the senses, emotions and experiences that the city has to offer, the transformation of something ordinary and familiar into something unexpected.

Walking and recording are used to unearth stories that live in the locations being traversed, which may be factual or fictional or more likely a combination of both. Walking can be a group activity, think 'walk-shop', or a solitary one. Often perceived as a political act, on foot, a walker can go against the grain, veer off the well-trodden track, explore the overlooked and the peripheral, and present a challenge to the perceived organisation of the city. Increasing privatisation of the urban environment, often unseen, means that walking is an increasingly complex activity and potentially, overtly political. City walking or wandering has become a dominant feature of this type of research, although this method is not exclusive to urban locations and can be used to investigate a variety of landscapes. Psychogeography can be used not just as an end in itself, but also as a tool for larger political or cultural investigations that result in effective change which have impact on these environments.

Documentation of the act of walking often appears as a form of map-making; when inventive in nature, it can provide alternative and innovative readings of space and time. David Lemm, whose work is often interactive or collaborative, uses iconography found in cartography and wayfinding to record the personal or historical. Whether retracing lost routes across the Isle of Eigg or examining redevelopment in London's Kings Cross area, Lemm uses the map form to record narratives or memories, while exploring and subverting map-making visual languages and conventions.

DEBRIS AND PHENOMENA
David Lemm

Based on a series of walks around Edinburgh, these screenprints feature symbolic representations of the built environment. The images suggest a cityscape that is fluid, fragile and unstable; mysterious icons float above indiscernible measurements and codes that exist on the found admiralty charts Lemm uses to print onto. A workshop hosted by Lemm invited participants to create their own 'maps' by following a prescribed route and encountering ink stamps at various locations along the way.

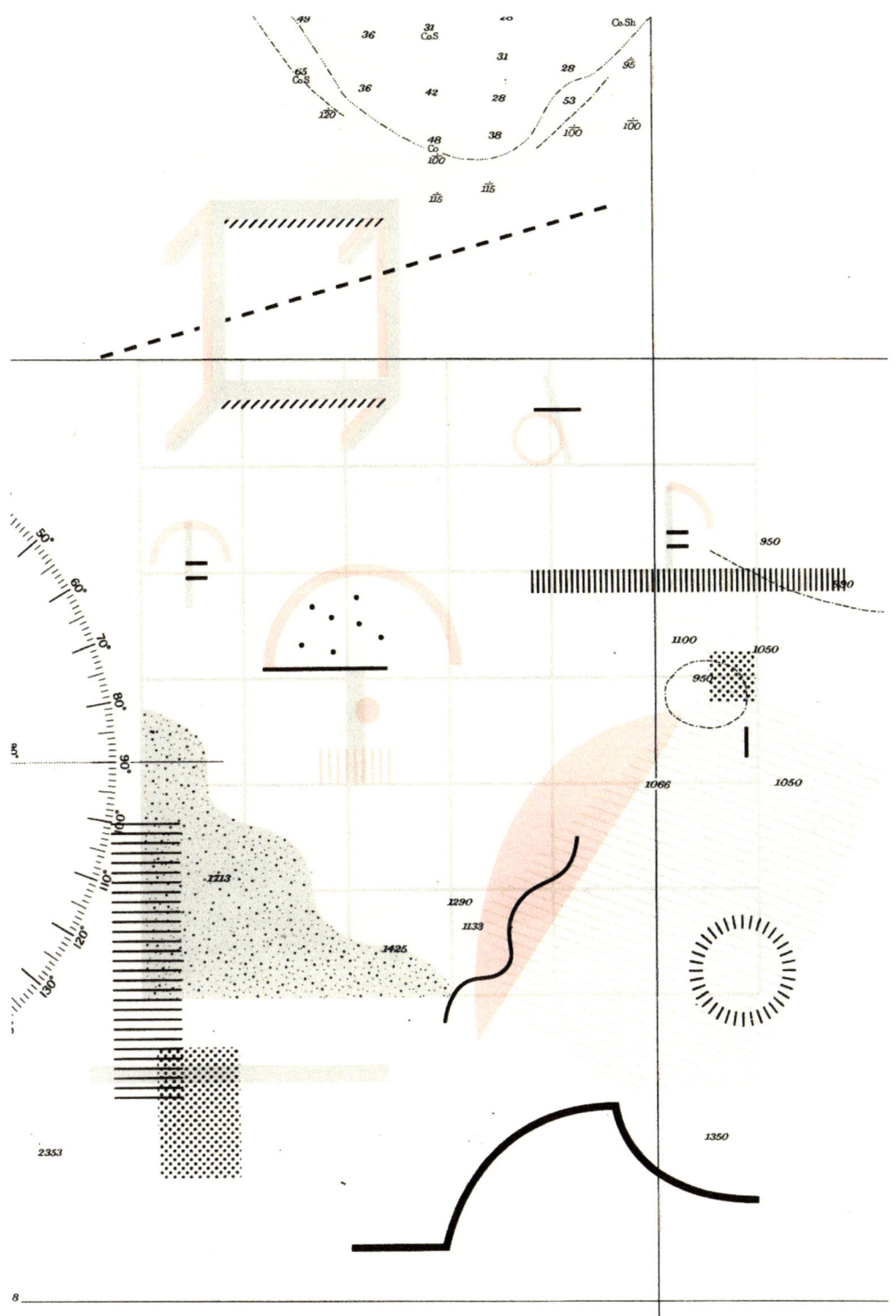

DEBRIS AND PHENOMENA
David Lemm

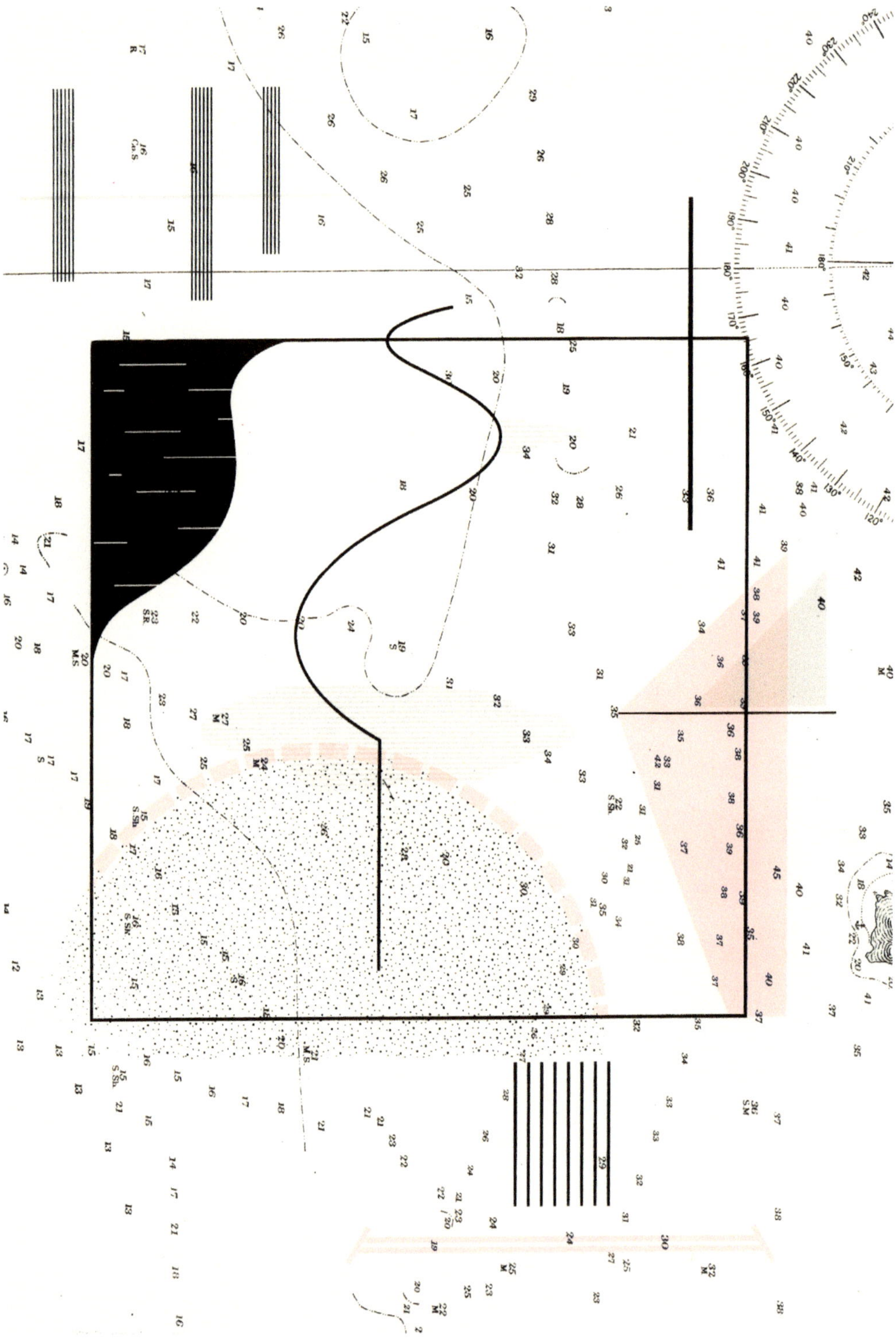

DIALECTOGRAMS
Mitch Miller

 From a distance, these drawings appear as a tangle of information; orthographic projections of buildings, copious notes, comic panels and plans jostle for the viewer's attention. On closer reading, the data is revealed and stories unfold. What appears resembles an intense discussion or commentary. These *dialectograms* produced by illustrator Mitch Miller combine psychogeographic and anthropological research methods in order to document and preserve locations that are to be demolished, usually within politically or socially sensitive situations. The Red Road estate in Glasgow is one such area. Built in the fervour of post-war Britain and demolished by 2016, this site represents the continuing rise of privatisation and a distinctly neo-liberalist agenda. By talking to those affected and recording the ensuing commentary and conversations, Miller layers the subjective and the objective in a schematic representation of the location.

Multiple perspectives are documented, a premise fundamental to much social research, which assumes that there is always more than one way of looking at, or talking about, things; there is not one rational or correct way and that all attitudes and behaviours are based on social and cultural circumstances. These rough drawings deliberately distance themselves from the singular authority of architectural diagrams or town plans and instead, Miller becomes facilitator or recorder, developing a rapport with those he meets, attempting to understand how they view their own world. The resulting images are a complex network or meshwork of relationships. As the layers of information become more complex, there is the potential for the imagery to become less explicit, and to demand more of the reader. Keen to understand what 'participation' or 'working with' means within the practice, Miller is acutely aware of the need to understand exactly who benefits from this type of practice. With a practice that often edges towards activism or the socially engaged, questions regarding participation and audience are always at the fore. Often made 'on-site', on completion the *dialectograms* are reproduced and returned to the location in which they were made in order to be used by residents, city planners or local authorities.

Flâneur (masculine) and Flâneuse (feminine)

A person who navigates and contemplates the urban environment through the act of leisurely wandering.

Psychogeography

An interdisciplinary field of inquiry most overtly bringing together psychology and geography, used to experience and navigate the city, urban and natural environments. Associated with the Situationist International organisation.

DIALECTOGRAMS
Mitch Miller

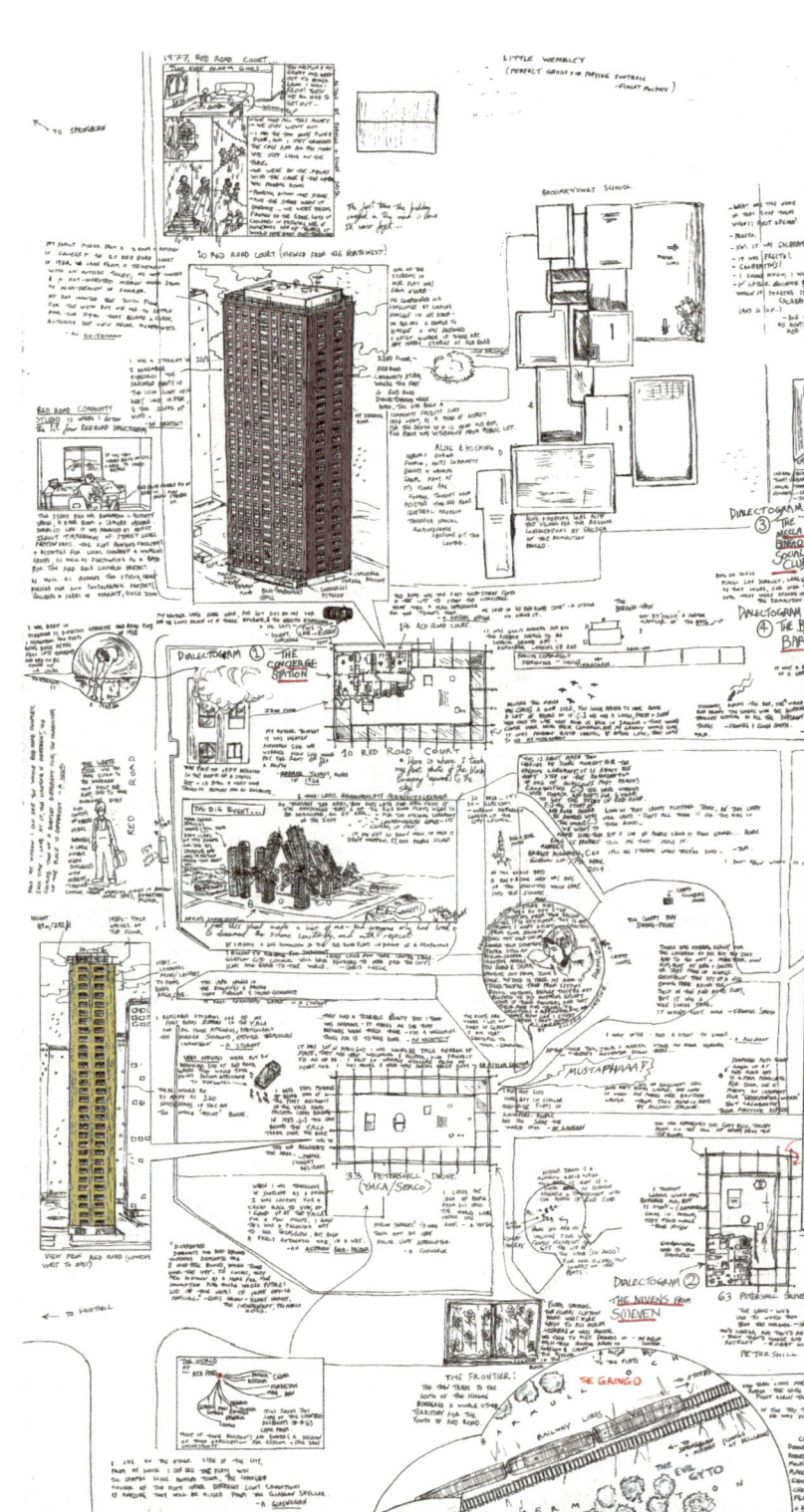

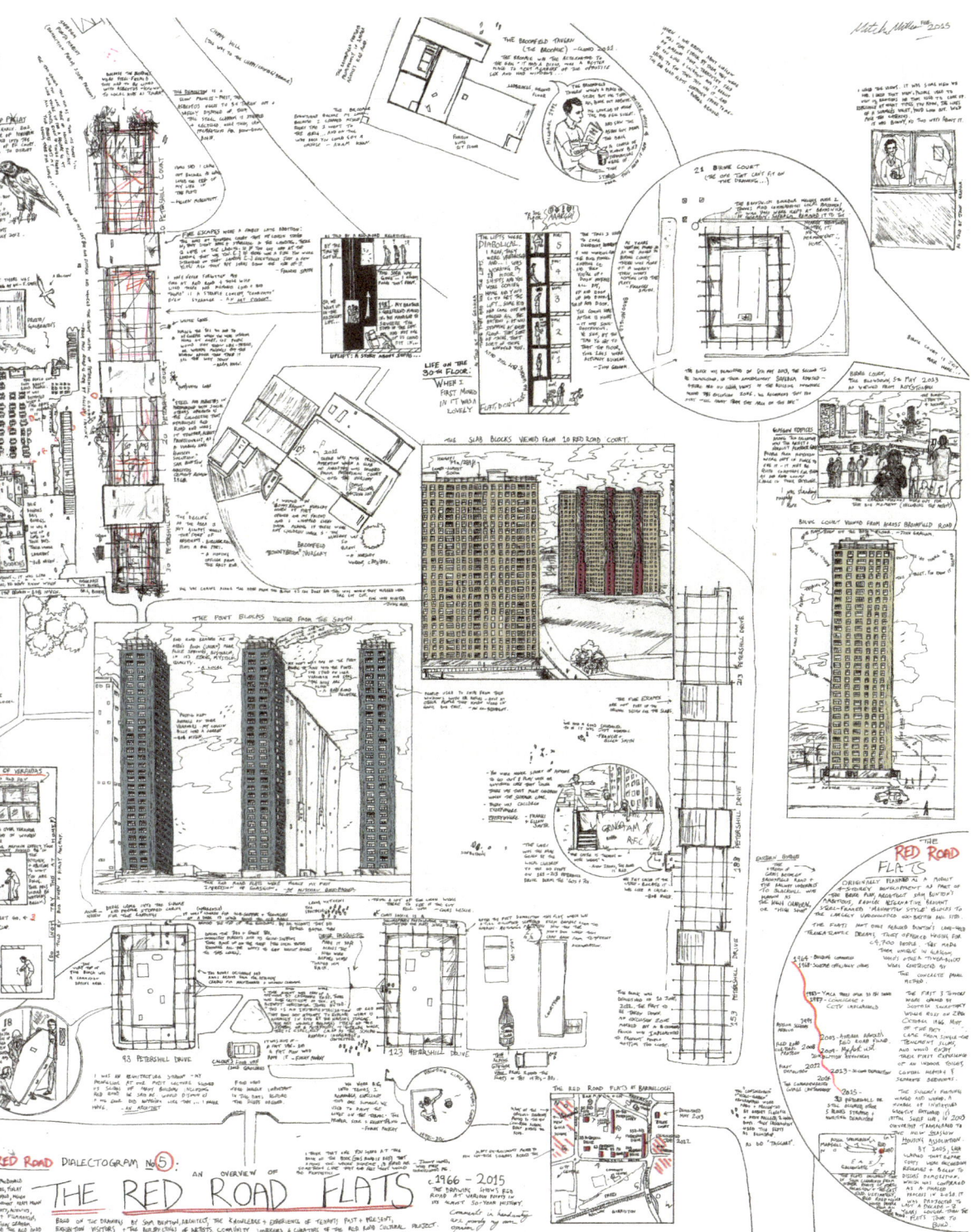

AN ALTERNATIVE ARCHIVE
OF BRUTALIST ARCHITECTURE:
2008-2018
Gareth Barnett

Cyberspace, or more specifically Google Maps, provides an augmented version of the 'real' world in which to travel. The 'street view' function on Google Maps gives us the opportunity to wander the streets of almost any country in the world. Gareth Barnett has reframed Situationist methods, such as the dérive, and has roamed these virtual streets. In his work *An Alternative Archive of Brutalist Architecture: 2008-2018*, Gareth Barnett uses these research methods to record the political and ideological legacy of Brutalist Architecture. Despite its systematic destruction in the real world, brutalist 'ruins' still exist in the virtual world and these are 'grabbed' and archived. These are all buildings that no longer exist in the physical world but can now be accessed through Google Street View. The four walks are Robin Hood Gardens, Leeds International Swimming Pool, Barnsley Metropolitan Centre and The Trinity Centre Multi-storey Car Park. Familiar research methods are adapted and augmented to investigate specific contemporary cultural phenomena.

Dérive

A psychogeographical method in which a journey through an urban terrain is made on foot, guided only by emotional psychological impulses and encounters.

Me, you and everyone else

It is impossible to switch off any preconceived views, motives and definitions when entering into any new situation, and that subjectivity is impossible to overcome completely. This can be mitigated by a thorough reflection of your own individual perspective and viewpoint. When working with others, never assume we all share the same knowledge. The real world is messy, and people's experiences, perspectives and opinions will vary.

There are diverse ways of navigating through and processing our circumstances and environments, within any given situation there will be a multitude of narratives at play. When a researcher enters into a scene they, too, inform and influence the dynamics at play. Attention must be paid to the power relationships at play between the researcher and what or whom is being observed. Biases and prejudices may be unconscious or bound within accepted norms. This operates both ways.

Consider what you represent to others through your immediate visual identity, for example: age, gender, race, physical presence, clothing, etc. What is perceived by the researcher is informed by a multitude of factors, for example: education, personal background, heritage, memories, etc. How the researcher is perceived will also influence how others present and portray themselves. This needn't discourage the research process, nor imply that the response must be impartial. Instead, recognise that the presence of the researcher will impact on the situations they place themselves in and the subjects they document. The way we position ourselves should be appropriate to what we are trying to discover or record.

For the illustrator, positioning can be understood in a number of ways. Physical positioning, for example, when working from observation, recognising where you situate yourself can alter the social dynamics within the environment. Should you be known by your subjects, are you public-facing or a discrete voyeur, and what are the ethical implications within your decision-making?

The position of the researcher within the wider study is a necessary consideration, for example, what role do you occupy? Do you, for example, consider yourself an 'expert' or an 'authority figure'? Is there a predetermined stance or opinion you hold? What is informing your inquiry? Posing such questions to ourselves throughout our working processes can alert us to the dangers of 'othering'; portraying or treating people as different, lesser or unfamiliar to ourselves and what we understand as the norm.

NORTHEYE
Leah Fusco

Illustration methods can be used to document an event that has happened in the far-distant past. Leah Fusco's practice-based PhD research explores the documentation of *Northeye*, an abandoned medieval settlement located on Pevensey Levels, an area of marshland in East Sussex, England. Fusco's practice as an illustrator firmly nods to the tradition of the more familiar reportage or documentary movement, but steps further towards establishing the working process of the illustrator as a distinctive ethnography. Deeply embedded in research, Fusco is a hybrid practitioner drawing from a wide range of references such as critical art theory and research methodologies from counterpart subject areas such as geology and archaeology. Fusco's lens is distinctive in that she is a native of the landscape that has so often been the focus of her work. She does not immerse herself within the environment, she simply belongs to it, which allows her to communicate a tacit understanding of the place and its people – those who know and use the site: the cattle farmer, the shepherd, the archivist and the local historian. The narrative of Northeye described here is not linear, but then neither is its history. Its story has been shaped by a number of human factors and environmental interventions. It has had a multitude of different roles: a site of settlement, worship, crime, and agriculture – the ruins of which now exist as earthworks. This palimpsest of stories is encapsulated by Fusco's retelling; a web of narratives simultaneously looking to the past, present and future.

3 REPORTING

Me, you and everyone else

NORTHEYE
Leah Fusco

REPORTING

Me, you and everyone else

NORTHEYE
Leah Fusco

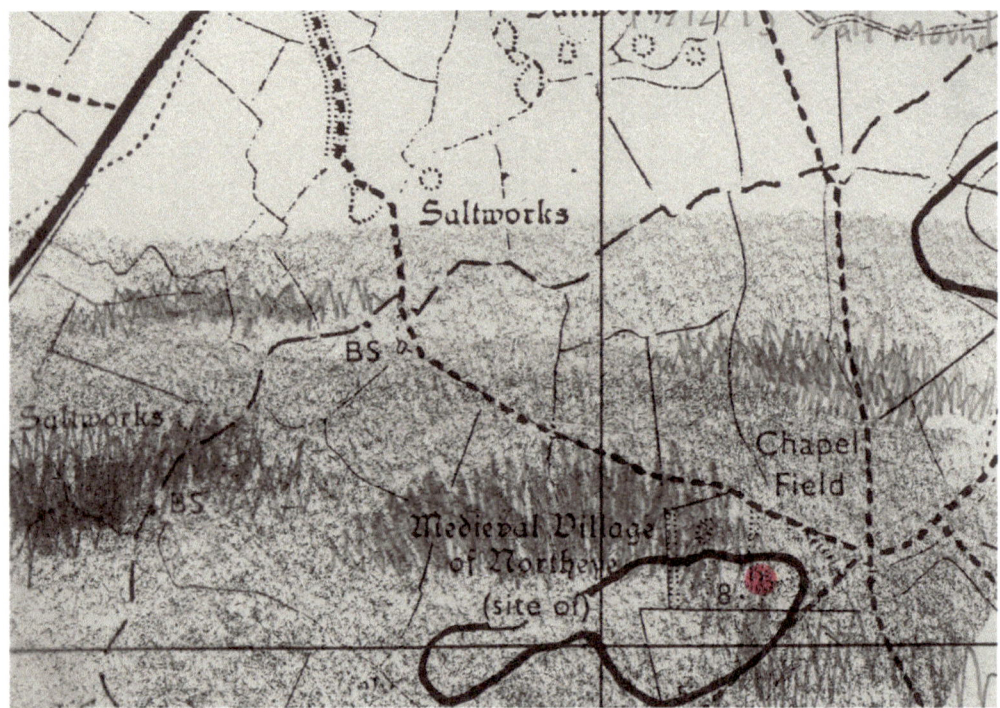

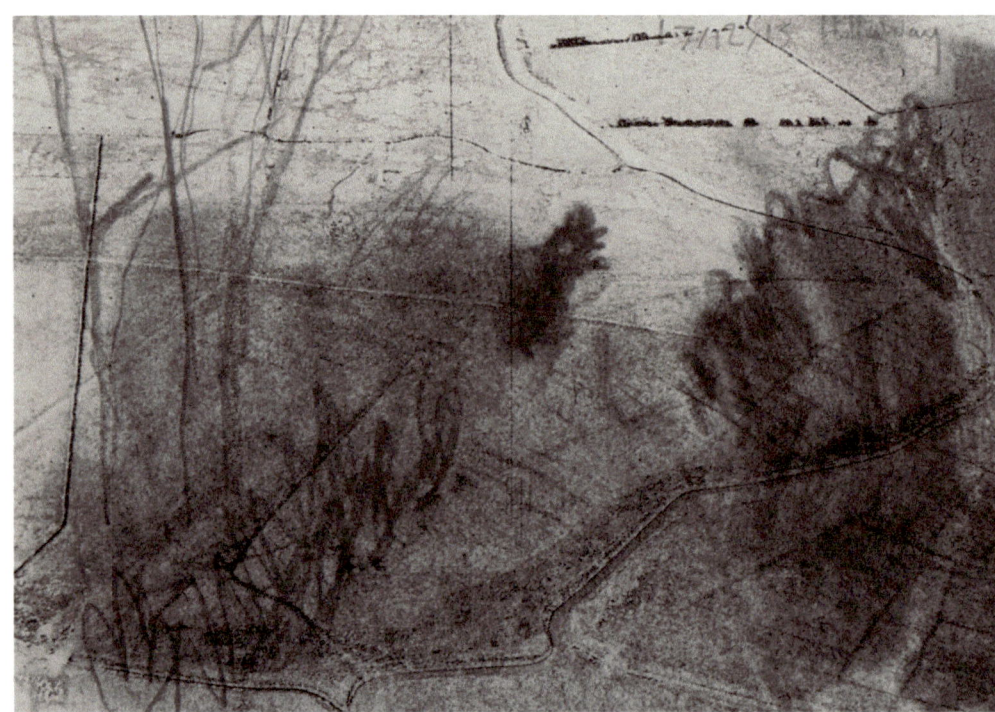

Is this real?

Being truthful or true to the facts of real events are common preoccupations for those working within documentary disciplines. The illustrator will be working with first-hand accounts (perhaps their own), witnesses and personal stories, and may be concerned that they are not directly representative of what actually exists; a true version of events that accords with facts or reality.

While this is a valid concern, truth and what is real are complex notions that require unpacking in relation to the discipline of illustration, which differs in its approach, principles and methods to documentary film-making or photojournalism, for example, which share similar concerns.

Consider first what it means to be truthful. In many courts of law, witnesses vow to tell the truth and evidence is presented as facts. A defendant is decreed guilty or innocent and this is then considered the true account of what occurred, only to be contested by those guilty parties who claim that they know the 'real' truth. As individuals, we occupy multiple identities, perform various roles socially and our comprehension of our past experiences is constantly evolving.

Myths and stories convey symbolic or fundamental truths; some of which are specific to certain cultures and disputed by others, while others are applicable to all human thought. We use these stories in order to make sense of events; to put them in an order that aligns with our view of the world. A very different kind of truth to the evidential kind, and yet no less 'truthful'. Therefore, we may take from this that there are multiple truths and no absolute or singular truth. How then can these ideas be understood within the framework of illustration practice? Fundamentally, illustration doesn't claim to represent reality, it is interpretive. In any case, it shouldn't be assumed that all the facts are accessible to the illustrator. Illustration is analytical, diagnostic and investigative. Illustrations explain, reveal and make clear. The role, or concern, of the illustrator therefore, is not to report the facts but instead to communicate so as the viewer understands, empathises or questions.

Reporting the news

Editorial illustration can provide the opportunity to discuss socio-political issues and current affairs. Traditionally reproduced in print formats, newspapers, journals and magazines were the typical mode of news delivery. Editorial illustration is responsive and often positioned alongside a piece of journalist writing. These images may be sympathetic to the content of this text, or offer a second opinion or additional insight, dependent on commissioning process, art director and/or publisher.

It is important to note that the editorial illustrator works within commissioned parameters. This doesn't necessarily imply a lack of freedom, as illustrators are often commissioned because of their distinctive visual identity or concern with particular subject matters. They will be working and negotiating with editors and publishers, who may have some influence on the aesthetic, content and emphasis of the illustration produced.

Today, sadly, we don't have to look far to be confronted with images of war, torture and death. The proliferation of such images of horror has done much to dull our senses when it comes to documentation of atrocities and trauma.

Ethnocentrism
The act of making pejorative or negative judgements of a perceived culture based on the observer's own preconceptions, values and world view.

Illustration has the ability to defamiliarise subject matter when tackling overly familiar content, to make an audience see something as if for the first time. Other image-making methods have this ability, of course, but their overabundance and infiltration into all forms of media mean that they have arguably lost some of their ability to shock or surprise.

Along with other news media, editorial illustration is going through a revolution, straddling print, corporation news websites and social media platforms. As news content is increasingly consumed online, publishing outlets are adapting their operations to fully utilise the opportunities offered by the digital world. This in turn has presented new possibilities for editorial illustration, which can now be produced for a range of different screen-based media. A field of work that would have at one point in history been entirely print-based now encompasses interactive and moving content: games, animations and films. This potential for interaction and moving image should be seen not simply as a novelty, a way of hooking in distracted readers, but as a way to 'animate' those stories or voices that perhaps could not otherwise be heard, or those that require a 'telling' that is abstracted and less overtly representational.

GUANTÁNAMO DIARY:
RENDITION, TORTURE AND
DETENTION WITHOUT CHARGE
Chris Clarke (Deputy Creative Director), Bill Bragg (Illustration) and Alexander Purcell (Motion Designer)
A video documentary for *The Guardian*

Guantánamo Diary is a short documentary film about Mohamedou Ould Slahi's declassified memoir, of the same name, and the extraordinary eight-year journey from its inception inside the US detention facility to worldwide publication. The part-animated, part-live action documentary was made for UK newspaper, *The Guardian online* to run alongside the serialisation of the book, and features the work of illustrator Bill Bragg.

The film presents multiple voices: the expert, the solicitor, the editor, the brother. Photography, interviews, testimony and illustration are seamlessly brought together. Bragg's illustrations take the voice of the author, Mohamedou Ould Slahi, whose memoir can be heard recounted over Bragg's depictions.

Rather than being a secondary accompaniment, illustration has been specifically employed to recreate the 'unphotographable' for reasons of security, secrecy or law. It is here that illustration enables us to 'see' and have empathy with an experience impossible to document in any other way. The use of interpretative imagery rather than the vivid reproduction of photography or film is particularly effective in offering a certain 'distance' from the highly descriptive accounts of torture. Much is communicated through atmosphere; the imagery is suggestive and implicit, allowing the viewer to sustain engagement with incredibly traumatic subject matter. Textural and monochromatic, the visual aesthetic distinctively belongs to Bragg, who moves into realms of moving image with ease. The animation is subtle; at times revealed only through the slightest movement of minuscule details – the moving of a pencil in the hand or flecks of dust in the air. The assured stillness and contemplative melancholy that is present throughout Bragg's wider body of illustrative work has been perfectly applied to communicating this traumatic testimonial. Bragg's rendering of the *Guantánamo Diary* showcases the new possibilities that are now available to the illustrator working as reporter. Not only does it challenge the age-old arguments regarding the hierarchy between text and image, but it also addresses issues around truth, the unseen and the believability of images.

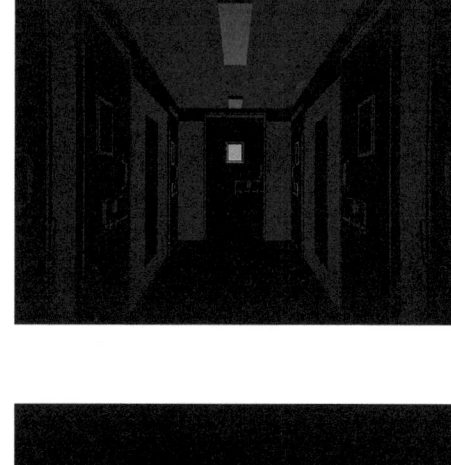

Othering

The creation of a psychological divide between the concept of 'us' and 'them' through recognition of an observed or imagined difference between individuals or social groups.

GUANTÁNAMO DIARY: RENDITION, TORTURE AND DETENTION WITHOUT CHARGE
Chris Clarke (Deputy Creative Director), Bill Bragg (Illustration) and Alexander Purcell (Motion Designer)
A video documentary for *The Guardian*

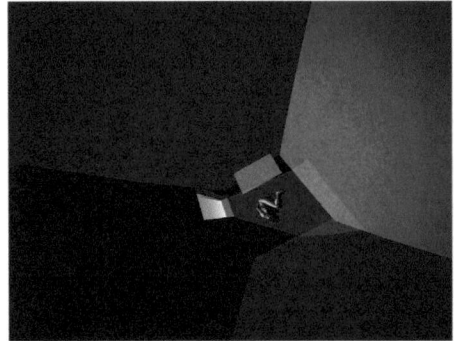

Decolonising movement

Discussion, debate and activism aiming to highlight, address and debunk the insidious effects of colonialism within the systems and hierarchies influencing our societal and cultural institutions.

4 CRAFTING

104 — Illustration and craft: a happy marriage?
— 'I already know what I'm going to do'
105 — The meaning in the mark
107 — Tools of the trade
110 — The meaning of material
114 — The stuff of life
121 — Illustration as object, 3d, physical and virtual form
126 — The illustrated object or the object illustration?
— Collected
— Fabricated
131 — Immaterial technologies

CONTEMPORARY ILLUSTRATION PRACTICE
IS CONCEPTUALISED,
CONSTRUCTED AND USED
WITHIN AN EXPANDING SET OF
CONDITIONS.
ITS EMERGENCE AS A
DISTINCTIVE DISCIPLINE HAS,
AND WILL CONTINUE TO BE,
INFORMED BY TECHNOLOGICAL
ADVANCEMENTS.

Illustration and craft: a happy marriage?

Contemporary illustration practice is conceptualised, constructed and used within an expanding set of conditions. Its emergence as a distinctive discipline has, and will continue to be, informed by technological advancements; printing, digital publishing, screen-based platforms, virtual realities, etc. Despite this, direct and tactile engagement with materials, making and technique are still considered central to good practice and inform much of an illustrator's education. This, met with the understanding that illustration is an applied art form, its inherent functionality, decorative leanings and audience inclusivity, has meant the discipline has enjoyed a relatively comfortable relationship with craft. However, historical associations with folk culture, nostalgia and emphasis on appearance over concept has coloured how craft-based skills are perceived within illustration. Does embracing craft-like similarities serve to reduce illustration's artistic status or might it offer an opportunity to showcase illustration's unique ability to occupy an elusive liminal territory where conceptual, accessible and functional creative practices can flourish?

'I already know what I'm going to do'

This phrase is a paradox: in the act of making, ideas develop and change. This is part of the process of development, it can't be prevented and shouldn't be feared. Regardless of how imminent the deadlines, time should be allocated to allow for this integral part of the process. Even very short deadlines will include an experimental preparatory stage during which a theoretical idea becomes a visual or physical reality. The more time available, the greater the opportunity for exploration. The initial idea of how a project might be visualised may seem like the definite and only resolution, but only actualising this idea will prove this indefinitely.

The visual exploratory stage of a project should begin as soon as an idea for a visual outcome arises. There is no 'right' time to begin working visually; theoretical and/or visual research and practical making can occur in synthesis and inform one another. Regardless of the medium of the process in use, there is a cognitive process in operation during the act of production. This is when the intellectual becomes manifest and can be critically evaluated in a way a theoretical idea cannot because it has no physical or visual form. It is in the act of testing, visual experimentation, working with materials and media that the illustrator interrogates the subject matter through a process of creative making. This acts as a kind of prototyping, testing through making, questioning the properties and possibilities of materials through actively engaging with them.

The conceptual subject matter is physically embodied and known through physical interaction. There is some form of human physical engagement in the process of making, regardless of how illustrative outcomes are articulated; the 'felt' touch of the materiality in a hand-rendered process, digital works are still human dependent for programming, operating software, etc. Audiovisual, performative works and time-dependent work may rely on a range of senses and faculties: voice, hearing, movement etc. The process of creative making is an integral research method, it does not only serve to articulate a final illustrative outcome, but is a form of creative investigation through which the illustrator better knows their subject matter and devises new, inventive or distinctive ways of practising illustration.

The meaning in the mark

The identity of an illustrator is often distinguishable by the appearance of their work, and this is particularly beneficial in order to maintain a public/professional presence and ensure exposure to support a commissioned career. However, even when an illustration is presented anonymously and/or the circumstances surrounding the realisation of the project are unknown, there still may be little clues imbedded within the work that reveal details about the individual who produced them. For example, mark-making not only reveals the impression of a gestural mark on a page but describes the weight and tension between the drawing instrument and the substrate; i.e. the consistent line of a technical pen describes the carefully controlled pressure of the hand that rendered the line, as well as the concentration needed to achieve such accuracy.

The materials and processes that illustrators use inform not only the appearance, but also the physical and emotional feeling. In this regard, they influence and have a voice within the work. Illustrations may be directly dictated by the materials used to create them, for example a print taken from a woodcut will reveal much more than just the images inscribed on the surface; it will also reveal the density of the wood; the direction of the grain; the type of tool used to make the cut and the pressure applied to make the print. All of these factors influence the visual outcome as well as what is being graphically depicted.

I AM A MESS, BUT SO ARE YOU.
LOVE, UTOPIA
Sandra Sordini

Human-sized, soft, flesh-toned figures lie sprawled in a carefully curated space to invite the interaction necessary for this multisensory narrative experience. The cushioned bodies can only lie flat, the plumpness begging to be touched, squeezed, coddled. Audio emanates from their chests with levels kept low to ensure that closeness is needed in order to hear. Lying in a head-to-chest embrace, the audience is engaged in a solo experience listening to voices recount intimate stories of sexual experiences.

The Bauhaus

Art school where founder Walter Gropius (1883-1969) and his peers reimagined art and design education with the intention to break down barriers and hierarchies between art and craft, and to engage with industrial production techniques.

I AM A MESS, BUT SO ARE YOU.
LOVE, UTOPIA
Sandra Sordini

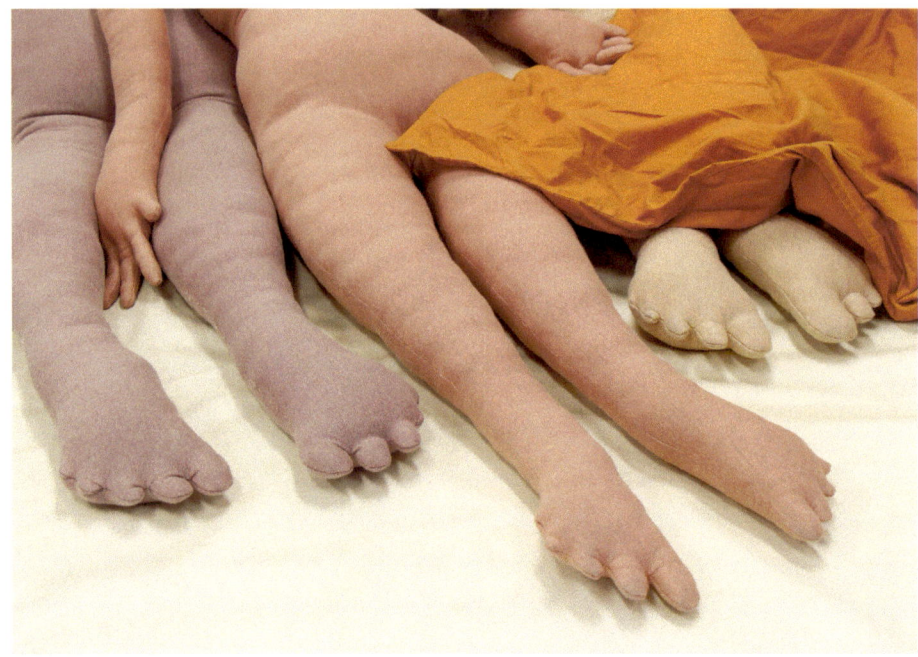

Tools of the trade

While illustration might be most familiar within 2d printed formats, it can take any form or be produced with any single or combination of media. This diversity makes it difficult to define illustration by its material properties, or to generalise the apparatus through which it has been produced. Tools will be particular to the individual illustrator, the brief and/or the task at hand. Methods are also context-specific, for example: working from a desk space in a communal environment may better suit a screen-based practice, and drawing on location, where wet media is prohibited, will dictate working with dry materials.

Tools serve to both extend and limit the possibilities of what is created. There are the tools of creation; the materials and equipment associated with the production of illustration. These may be informed by personal preference and training; i.e. a printmaker and their favourite linocutting tool. The concept of the project or a commissioner might dictate how the work should be made or the means of production may be defined by the materials and equipment you have access to at that particular time. Restrictions are not always a hindrance to quality, much can be achieved with limited means, and restrictions can provoke inventive and imaginative approaches. For example, hacking or reappropriating technologies. Consider the resurgence of the Risograph printer, now ubiquitous within independent publishing. Once used as an inexpensive way to mass-produce leaflets and pamphlets, the distinctive grainy image and the rudimentary print settings and functions have been widely experimented with to achieve textures, patterns and colour overlays, which are now recognised as printed artworks in their own right. 'Tools' can also extend what is possible and enable new ways of conceiving illustration. For example, collaborations open opportunities to expand on individual expertise for more ambitious projects to be realised.

LIZZIE: STRIDING ALONG
Amy Goodwin

The fairground, its people, culture and customs are not only symbiotic within the work of illustrative storyteller and signwriter Amy Goodwin, but are also deeply imbued within her own personal history. Raised among a fairground community, summers were spent travelling the English West country with her family while her father, owner of a steam engine, worked to power the travelling steam fairs.

Navigating a dual professional identity, Goodwin's occupation as a signwriter is distinct and independent from her illustration practice, yet her highly specialist skill set effortlessly traverses the two. More at ease positioning her practice in relation to craft, Goodwin describes illustration and craft as often distinct but with potential for union. Giving an example in relation to her own specialism, she explains, signwriters were not conscious of, or even interested in illustration; they were craftspeople performing a task necessary within their industry. Historically, signwriting struggled to be considered an art form and instead occupied a reduced status as craft. This is, in part, linked to its functional application; it being a taught skill and a paid-for service. Signwriting, Goodwin explains, is not traditionally about interpretation but is governed by restraint. As a commissioned signwriter independent of her illustrative practice, much of Goodwin's work involves conserving and restoring steam engines where there is limited space for individual expression. However, her creative work plays on how restraint and the

<u>Tangibility</u>
Having actual material substance rather than being imaginary or speculative.

4 CRAFTING

Tools of the trade

distinctive visual tropes associated with signwriting such as letter forms, shadow, colour and their connotations, can be used to portray, hold, tell and conceal narratives. Goodwin's transition into illustration practice followed after her training as a professional signwriter. Her training, in the manner of a traditional apprenticeship with Carters Steam Fair, required two additional years of practice and application, as is customary, to reach professional standard.

At this point, Goodwin entered into the MA in Authorial Illustration programme at Falmouth School of Art, UK to hone her skills within an academic structure. Proposing to use the vocabulary and aesthetics of signage to relate a story about a travelling fairground, Goodwin identified the course specifically because of its emphasis on authorial narrative and experimental practice. Within illustration she could apply her technical ability within a conceptual framework. The post-graduate project ultimately led Goodwin toward her doctoral research, re-establishing identities of fairground females while exploring how this medium and visual aesthetic, indivisible with fairground culture, could be used to comment on its own history. The signs Goodwin creates within her doctoral illustration practice are, in their unique form, the conduits of narrative. Often presented within exhibitions, the works are accompanied by catalogues that describe a more overt narrative. Goodwin regards these texts as independent but enriching to the experience of encountering the signs. They serve as triggers prompting the audience to look more closely and decode the messages implicit within the individual visual elements.

LIZZIE: STRIDING ALONG
Amy Goodwin

The meaning of material

The materials through which illustration is rendered convey meaning independent from the content of the information the work describes. Material properties communicate visually, as well as through tactility, and the full gamut of bodily senses reachable in an audience.

The methods and media that illustrators use belong to the canon of design and art history, which also influence how the illustration is read. For example, a drawing made using charcoal, a woodcut and a digital photographic collage will all have different connotations and make reference to different historic time frames or art movements, which can influence the overall meaning of the work.

Illustration often only reaches an audience once reproduced. The original artwork as made by the hand of the illustrator, regardless of means of production, is seldom encountered or showcased. A zine, a cloth-bound book and a mobile phone screen all have the potential to showcase or contain the same illustrative work, but their vastly different properties will heavily impact how the illustration will communicate. The act of reproduction alters the material qualities and value of the work; unique and distinctive artefacts are transformed into reproduced or ephemeral copies. When used with awareness, any material associations or connotations can be utilised to consolidate relationships, make statements or highlight conceptual links. Media, materials and methods of dissemination always influence meaning.

CONCRETE
Daise Rowe

An ipad displays a sequence of animated graphite marks, rubbings and textures. As the impressions flit and mutate across the screen, a steadily voiced monologue delivers poetic ponderings on the ubiquitous construction material: concrete.

'... Expands, retracts, press, hold, move on, scruitinise the perplexion; the concrete, the not.'

Original drawings and more texts, some of which have been bound together into simple publications, accompany the animation. The choice of materials is specific and deliberate, as is the calm tone and pacing of the audiovisual piece. The paper stock is light and crisp, and the choice of typeface is subdued, allowing the grainy texture of the graphic marks to be uncompromised. The slight translucency of the paper reveals just a hint of what has gone before and is yet to come. Also presented are small casts of physical concrete that you are invited to touch. The audience encounters multiple communication strategies simultaneously, all the while negotiating these enigmatic illustrative interpretations that defamiliarise a material so commonplace in everyday life.

For Daise Rowe, the fascination with concrete lies in the tension between its pragmatic functionality and its use as a linguistic metaphor to describe that which is known and consolidated. Herein lies the paradox; once set, the final form is permanent, but before this point concrete is highly malleable. It transitions from powder, to liquid, to solid substance. A composite in dry powder form, its final strength, appearance and texture can be manipulated by altering ratios and adding ingredients such as aggregates or rocks. Concrete is also extremely responsive when cast, and when set, it will adopt the shape and texture of the mould into which it has been poured. Rowe emphasises the importance of working with the material early on, in order to directly experience and observe how the material performs. Handling and controlling concrete also allowed for a physical, tactile understanding, which Rowe explains helped form a connection to the resulting physical form, which can sometimes be lacking when you are absent from the process of its creation.

Rowe also researched more broadly, making contact with other specialists also using concrete in their fields of work, stressing collaboration and knowledge exchange as important. Rowe understands that while something new and interesting can result from experimentation, being knowledgeable with a working process and understanding how things are done properly is important. During the project, Rowe met and exchanged ideas with an architecture student, who shared his particular experience of using concrete as a construction material. Rowe explains, because concrete is so widely used there are many avenues that can be taken, and through having conversations you are able to gain more insight than might otherwise be possible.

The eponymously titled 'Concrete' is an illustrative inquiry, drawing together Rowe's various creative analyses. Rowe stresses the importance of the participatory experiential element of the work, which breaks down the formality of any gallery space. Audiences should touch and hold concrete while viewing the film, that multiple engagement of sight, hearing and physical sensation is absolutely necessary to gain an overall understanding. Rowe frequently uses touch as an illustrative devise to communicate, explaining that it triggers an emotional response particularly when the piece of work is fully or in part object based; there is a curiosity, a connectivity – do you feel what I feel?

Aura

Coined by philosopher Walter Benjamin (1892-1940) as a quality relating to a presence in time and space, intrinsic within original artworks and impossible to capture through means of mechanical reproduction.

CRAFTING

The meaning of material

CONCRETE
Daise Rowe

112

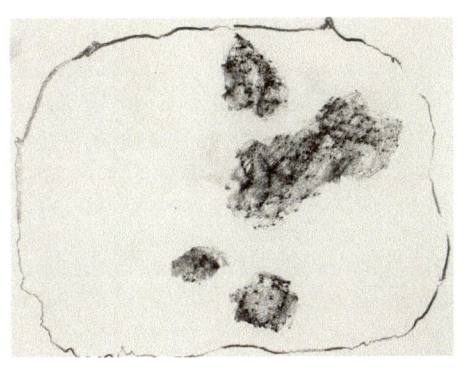
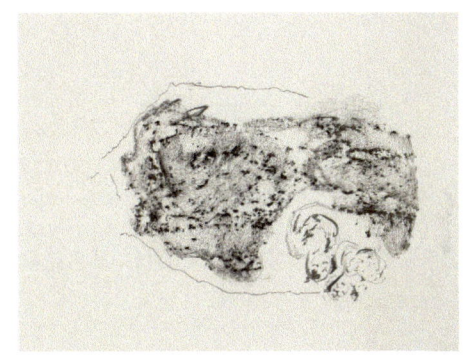
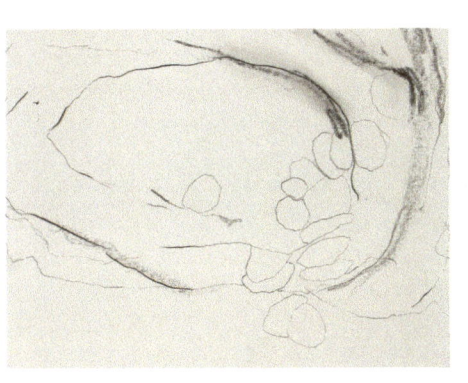

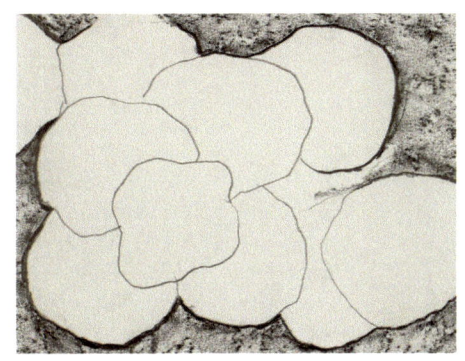

The stuff of life

A readymade component incorporated within an illustrative work brings a rich source of detail that will inform what and how the work communicates. Objects resonate with concepts, knowledge and narratives. Even when defunct or removed from obvious human use they are able to convey meanings and messages that transcend their immediate applications and contexts. They are evocative of social and cultural relationships that refer to their previous human associations, for example, a pair of glasses is not only a vision aid but is able to capture a sense of the individual who once wore them; clues to their identity, gender, personality traits and the historical time period they lived in. Objects can also reflect broader historical narratives through reflecting the social, historical and political circumstances that lead to their original conception, production and use. Design, materials and methods of manufacture can speak of bygone industries, skills, communities and political dynamics. For example, the Brown Betty teapot may not only be understood as a ubiquitous English kitchen utensil but could also be evocative of the domestic environment where it is often found. It could also be understood as a representation of the cultural specific ritual of tea drinking; the heritage of a near lost national cottage industry or refer to a history of colonisation.

Objects can become associated with identities and desires quite removed from their original intended purpose, through being appropriated or assigned meaning to a particular cultural or subcultural group. These associations might not be immediately apparent or explicit and can be used to communicate between those belonging within a particular collective or community. Contexts and modes of dissemination will also add and contribute to the audience understanding. Objects associated with particular communities, liferoles, environments or activities might be rendered unfamiliar and invite new readings when encountered in unfamiliar situations. Through understanding the narrative potential of objects, illustrators can consider how multiple forms can be brought together to form new meanings through association. These associations might be an entirely new physical form constructed from various recognizable components. Such a work may highlight tensions or affiliations and/or create meaning inferred by the composite elements. Objects, things and artefacts might also be drawn together through a form of assembly or curation where their physicality, as found by the illustrator, is unaltered, but a narrative is informed through the associations created by their juxtaposition.

TOOLS FOR LIVING
Jasleen Kaur

Jasleen Kaur creates sculptural forms that fuse together objects from the everyday to make new hybrid forms, highlighting cultural tensions and cohesions. Informed by her personal history as a Sikh woman born and raised in Glasgow, Kaur's choice of materials are often culturally specific, referencing the domestic environment and speaking of migrant identity and aspiration.

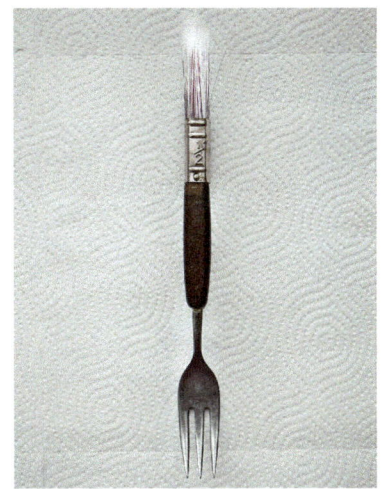

Medium is the message

A concept suggested by philosopher Marshall McLuhan (1911–1980), which states that the media used as the vehicle of delivery more profoundly impacts and affects society than the message it attempts to portray.

THE IN-BETWEEN: AN ODE TO EPPING FOREST
Rachel Lillie

Epping Forest, rambling from east London into the Essex countryside, is now dissected by motorways and the encroaching conurbations. This ancient woodland contains areas of grassland, heath, rivers, bogs and ponds, and has been continually forested since Neolithic times. Home to two Iron Age earthworks, Queen Elizabeth's Hunting Lodge and granted the title of the 'People's Forest' by Queen Victoria, this area of suburban London is as rich with history as it is flora and fauna. Illustrator Rachel Lillie makes these 2,400 hectares the focus of her project *The In-between: An Ode to Epping Forest*.

Lillie considers her practice as sitting somewhere between the contemplative nature writing that has had a resurgence in recent years, and contemporary psychogeography in which practitioners use walking as a method to retrace and relive London histories. Cherishing the natural landscape, rather than the built environment, sets Lillie's practice apart from these urban wanderers, concerned that our increasingly urbanised lives have led to an almost complete disconnect with nature. With the Epping Forest project, Lillie aims to rediscover this connection for herself and in the process, encourages others to do the same.

The work is a combination of drawings made on location and objects carved or constructed from wood sourced in Epping Forest. These are displayed alongside archival material and field note sketchbooks at the Vestry House Museum located in the Epping Forest locale. This local museum is the intended context for this work, and it is in this setting that the work is fully realised.

Each of the wooden objects are aligned with a drawing of a specific location, acting as symbolic clues to past stories now concealed by the forest landscape depicted in the drawings. Some of these made artefacts reference actual historical objects, others the topography or man-made constructions long since disappeared: a hunting horn, a bomb crater or a deer shelter. An intuitive approach to the craft of wood carving has resulted in the surface of the objects having a naïve and textural quality, mimicking the pencil marks found in the drawings. An Iron Age pot has aged over time, the wood cracking and blackening as it dried; a transformation suggestive of the firing process of ceramics. A piece of wood carved to trace the path of a stream is reminiscent of the Ammassalik tactile wooden maps of the Greenlandic coastline, anachronistic and archaic. A radio mast made from sticks is an almost maquette-like reconstruction, primitive diagrams for structures that no longer exist.

Lillie's objects are not trickeries or fakes aiming to lead an audience to believe that these were in fact found; they are symbolic – hints at a past reconstructed. The process is one of reconstructing the past from fragments; and reminiscent of an archaeologist digging up material traces of history only to reconstruct them in order for us to visualise historical moments. This practice is commonplace in museums where the reconstructed parts of objects are made from different materials to that of the original fragments, and therefore stand out. Lillie stresses that the meaning is sought in the in-between, the space between the drawings and the objects; between present and past. We are asked to construct the histories ourselves from the clues. Lillie asserts these objects as distinctly illustrative – having no inherent function or usefulness, and are instead figurative, pictorial and narrative.

LONG RUNNING

4 CRAFTING

The stuff of life

**THE IN-BETWEEN:
AN ODE TO EPPING FOREST**
Rachel Lillie

DEER SHELTER PLAIN

STAPLES BROOK

THE IN-BETWEEN: AN ODE TO EPPING FOREST
Rachel Lillie

CHINGFORD PLAIN

Illustration as object, 3d, physical and virtual form

It is becoming increasingly familiar to find illustrators presenting works realised as objects, artefacts or sculptural forms. While there is a clear compulsion and ambition to operate within the physical and spatial domain, such works are not easily categorised and are multiple in their intentions, function and methods of production.

Considering illustration as an object or sculptural form raises some interesting questions. The first is a matter of terminology: is our current vocabulary apt to discuss such works and if not, what revisions are necessary? The second is a question of audience interaction; are these objects to be viewed, touched or used? The final question is a matter of mediation, as the methods of production, duplication and dissemination cannot be assumed. A unique object may be a form of artisanal craft-making or may be mass-produced as part of an industrialised production.

LANGUAGE   Literary terms are often used to discuss human interaction with illustration; audiences are described as readers, we discuss poetic images, and visual metaphors. This is easily rationalised and, arguably, is entirely justified considering the long-established understanding of illustration as pictorial narrative; its primary use to adorn literary texts and the printed word, and its frequent placement within book and publication formats. The reader of a literary text and a reader of illustration share much in common: they both decipher sequentially arranged visual codes into meaning, and are often physically engaging with literature and illustration in the same way – silently gazing and turning pages. While the rise of digital publishing has opened new opportunities, particularly for exploring motion and sound, the transition to screen has not greatly altered our conduct and processes of engagement. However, when we begin to consider illustration artefacts that transcend the 2d domain, either as a physical spatial form or within the realms of virtual environments, do these familiar terminologies remain valid? What vocabulary is then appropriate? Does the reader then become a user of illustration?

TO TOUCH OR NOT TO TOUCH   There is no denial that 2d illustration has material and tactile qualities that engage the senses and influence cognition. Consider the experience of touching a musty-smelling old book with brittle yellowing pages, the weight of it in your lap as you slowly turn the pages to view the illustrations within. You run your fingers across the image, feeling the decompressed surface resulting from the printing process. This full sensory encounter informs the reading of the illustrations. The same is true for any digital technology mediating the experience of illustration. The ambience created from presenting work on a wood-panel television set will be entirely different to that of the high-definition flat screen.

When an audience is confronted with an illustrative object, the physicality impacts the experience of engagement. Information is conveyed through touch, sensuous communication as well as visual experience. Illustration, understood as a process, suggests a temporal experience; the message emerges from a series of transitional encounters with a work of illustration. At what point does the illustrative object, thing or space become activated?

4 CRAFTING

Illustration as object, 3d, physical and virtual form

MEDIATED OBJECTS

Illustration is nearly always mediated; the original image, however constructed, is intended to be reproduced and viewed within another medium, conventionally in print or on-screen. This has been a defining characteristic of much illustration practice with its intrinsic and hereditary links to the print and media industries. The production of unique objects by illustrators transforms this dynamic. Such illustrative objects are no longer experienced in mediated form, instead the audience is asked to engage directly with the original artefact. In which case the public reach of the work is limited and the intended placement of the works (e.g, gallery, domestic, etc) has more significance as a place of encounter.

CROSSING TIME
Paddy Molloy

A proud spectacle stands in Central Square, at the heart of the newly developed King's Cross area of London; a giant projection screen framed within the most familiar architectural forms; the steeple, the arch, the gable roof and the perfect circle. Built from steel, the structure with its bold, clean lines is as evocative of modernity, construction and urban development as it is of the past, settlement and community.

The graphic shapes intersect one another creating a simple framed grid onto which randomised images are projected: cobbled stones, corrugated steel, a lifebuoy, stained glass, Romanesque pillars. The textures, artefacts and local details are visions of a rich history that look toward a potential future within a contemporary moment of rapid regeneration. *Crossing Time* speaks of tensions; tensions between the fleeting and the enduring, between what is known of a place and what is remembered, of what is gone and what is evidenced.

At four-metres tall, the installation is monumental, indeed it is an echo of a lost monument, that of the King's Cross statue of George IV, whose image can also been seen by canny eyes within the pictorial carousel. Best viewed by night, when set against the artificial glares of street lamps and perpetually lit business towers, the experience is theatrical and performative. At once static and time specific, each composition is unique as dictated by the randomising nature of the VJing software (VDMX) used to programme the display, and triggered by the movements of passers-by. Like a mirror reflecting the ceaseless evolution of the built environment, any visual record of the work is difficult to record for future posterity. Photography fails to capture the complexity of the work and any captured image serves to stabilise a narrative that is tirelessly mobile and forever at odds, shifting and constantly elusive.

Commissioned and facilitated by the House of Illustration in 2016, Molloy, responsible for conception, vision and creative direction, stresses this project was, in essence, entirely collaborative. Without a team of expert individuals, fabricators and technical consultants selected by Molloy, the work would have never realised its full ambition.

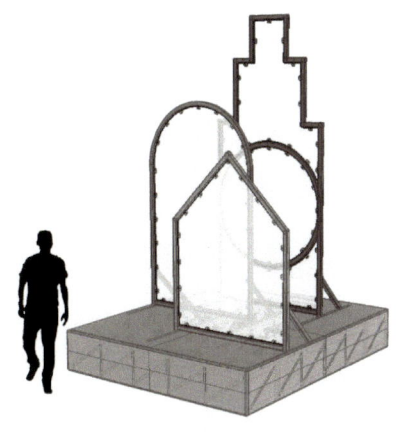

1
2
3

CRAFTING

Illustration as object, 3d, physical and virtual form

SPECIAL BODILY SENSATIONS
Kate Ducker

Kate Ducker's illustrative objects canonise the ephemeral debris of the traditions and social behaviours associated with drinking culture and celebratory customs. Cans of beer and bottles of alcopop, rendered in ceramic, appear much like votive offerings, while a life-sized perspex figure of a squatting woman surrounded by urine convey an observation of rituals that played part of the human state throughout time.

Tactility

The ability to be physically encountered and experienced through touch.

The illustrated object or the object illustration?

When illustration is applied to a physical form, for example, as surface pattern or decorative ornamentation, it prompts questioning of the status and position of the illustrative work within that object as a whole. Do we consider the communicative work of illustration as the wholly articulated object, say the curtain, or chair *or* is it the conduit through which the illustration is mediated? There is an important difference between these two suppositions. Illustration applied or incorporated onto 3d forms, for example, used within packing or product design, is very familiar. We enter into novel territory when the form is not merely the vehicle but is ingrained within how the communicative work of illustration operates. This subtle difference is monumental in readdressing hierarchies regarding intention and authorship; with the latter providing the illustrator with complete authorial freedom and authority (as opposed to the illustration as a commissioned component, where the intention and scope is likely defined by an external agent). The physicality of the illustrative work is not then implied as a secondary consideration but is instrumental in how the overall piece engages and communicates. The illustrator(s) may find themselves in the role of commissioners, sourcing skilled practitioners, such as craftspeople or engineers, to support the needs of the work. Here, the illustrated artefact may result with a singular unique object without any intention of being reproduced.

Collected

The activity of acquiring, storing and displaying collections is common practice among illustrators. Collections can be comprised of any imaginable content: objects, images, textures, artefacts, things found or made, discarded, functional, ornamental, domestic, historic, etc. The things we feel compelled to collect reveal something of our personal selves, they might be driven by a nostalgic longing, reinforce identities and affiliations and/or be driven by the thrill of acquisition and ownership. How illustrators use collecting and collections within their creative practices vary. Collections can act as repositories of ideas; curios becoming starting points for narrative investigations that develop into projects. Collections might be more directly used for creative production, for example print ephemera used for collage. The display of collections, particularly in the studio environment, might provide visual reference and allow for inspirational associations to be made. The act of collection is not limited to physical artefacts only. Digital programmes, online and social media platforms that allow data, such as photographs, images and texts to be organised, showcased and referred to, can also be understood as forms of collection.

Fabricated

Illustration is a social discipline, even if the production is performed alone, it is seldom the case that the practice of illustration will be entirely solitary. There are instances when the illustrator will need to work with others in order to create an intended outcome; it may require skills or expertise outside the remit of the illustrator, or the collaborative process or method of production may carry significance within the meaning of the work. Outsourcing manufacture does not always imply a bulk production; for example, employing a seamstress or bookbinder. This process will involve prototyping and the sourcing of materials and manufacturers, building relationships with those with differing knowledge or skills. The illustrator may find themselves instructing others; directing or coordinating production, and their 'hand' in the process may be invisible.

FROM SCRATCH
Laura Copsey

A miniature wheat field is growing in a portable metal container within the grounds of White City Place. A receipt itemises the most expensive loaf of bread, listing all the names of those whose help and knowledge was brought together to ensure this grain grew and stayed alive. Two tall hourglasses stand on plinths, passing steadily through the narrow apertures is soil and in the other, grain. Presented within this work, by Laura Copsey, aptly titled *From Scratch,* is also a corn wreath woven around a large rusted iron ring, a pair of millstone shoes and a carefully designed case containing bespoke tools and sundries for the practical and ritual cultivation and harvesting of the crop.

The realisation of Copsey's work never rests within a singular project or outcome, but instead within a series of interconnected events. This is a visual communication practice that manifests in various forms and incorporates a variety of collaborators. *From Scratch* takes grain as the focus to address the reoccurring themes prevalent within Laura Copsey's work, notably the subjective nature of history, collective identity, ritual and cyclical time.

Often the works are instigated and realised through 3d artefacts. Some objects are found while others are made by Copsey or with help from those with highly specialist skills, often belonging to lost traditions. Some of the artefacts that form Copsey's works are the result of collaboration; for example, the harvest toolkit was an inspired response from the product designer Philip Crewe, who donated the kit to be incorporated within the project as a whole. For Copsey, the collecting of objects and ephemera is an important research process. Some items are reclaimed having been discarded, others are bought second hand. The acquisitions are always found; happened upon, rather than sought out. Copsey explains that the attraction is impulsive and instinctive, and at the moment of discovery it isn't always known how these objects or things will come into play or inform a project. They are kept near in her home, lying within view but dormant, sometimes for years, before their significance comes to the fore.

The objects that preoccupy this practice are particular in that they are all artefacts that carry traces of human activity and invite speculation of lived experiences. Objects, particularly those whose provenance is unknown, invite speculation of how they were used, by whom and sometimes for what means. Copsey explains that objects are evocative of human history. They describe the things that people did, and their meaning is also accessible; they have a familiar presence that eliminates any hierarchy of understanding. Copsey favours the artefact object over the image, explaining that images imply a sense of permanence while objects are in flux, their uses and meaning apt to change with the passing of time. Objects invite participation, they encourage response through use and this engagement, which can serve to change the works or produce independent outcomes. Whole projects can be born from a chance finding. Copsey recalls a project stemming from a chance encounter with an abandoned ladder in a wood; the ladder called out to be climbed, its purpose defined it. The ladder went on to

Materiality
Relating to the physical and/or textural quality of the substances used in the production or constitution of an object, thing or artefact.

CRAFTING

Fabricated

inspire the creation of a fictional art collective formed of lumberjacks, to whom ownership of the ladder and other, invented, objects were attributed. This sense of humour and use of beguiling fiction is also distinctive of Copsey's practice. The fictional narratives surrounding Copsey's objects are communicated through their placement or the explanation of their origins. The millstone shoes appear as though they could be the relic of an agricultural process and would not be out of place within an ethnographic museum, yet they are a pure fabrication.

The spectacle of the piece was met with confusion as to its authenticity, creating a performative event in which the audience participate as they are drawn into the fiction. Here, the intention is not to trick or fool; the ridiculousness of the situation and the objects themselves intend to amuse. The discovery of the fiction is also part of the life cycle of the work. Often intentionally absurd or surreal, Copsey's artefacts are conceived with the intention of prompting conversations. The materials used to create them are highly considered. A number of works within *From Scratch* are made from bread; the process of making, baking and eating are as important as the physical appearance. One piece, a British Isles-shaped loaf, Copsey recounts, was particularly poignant in highlighting the uncomfortable nature of cutting and dividing the national regions, even in bread form.

Copsey's is a live, time and place specific communication practice. A practicing professional holistic therapist, Copsey positions herself in the role of a facilitator, organising and initiating events, workshops and collaborations. These social events, such as a bread-baking workshop or a field trip, are the realisation of the work, with the resulting documentation serving only as the debris of a unique experience. Within all Copsey's projects is an urgency to record and measure time: the live happening, the growing wheat, the flow of grain within the bespoke hourglasses and analogue audiovisual tape recordings are all temporal markers.

FROM SCRATCH
Laura Copsey

CRAFTING

Fabricated

FROM SCRATCH
Laura Copsey

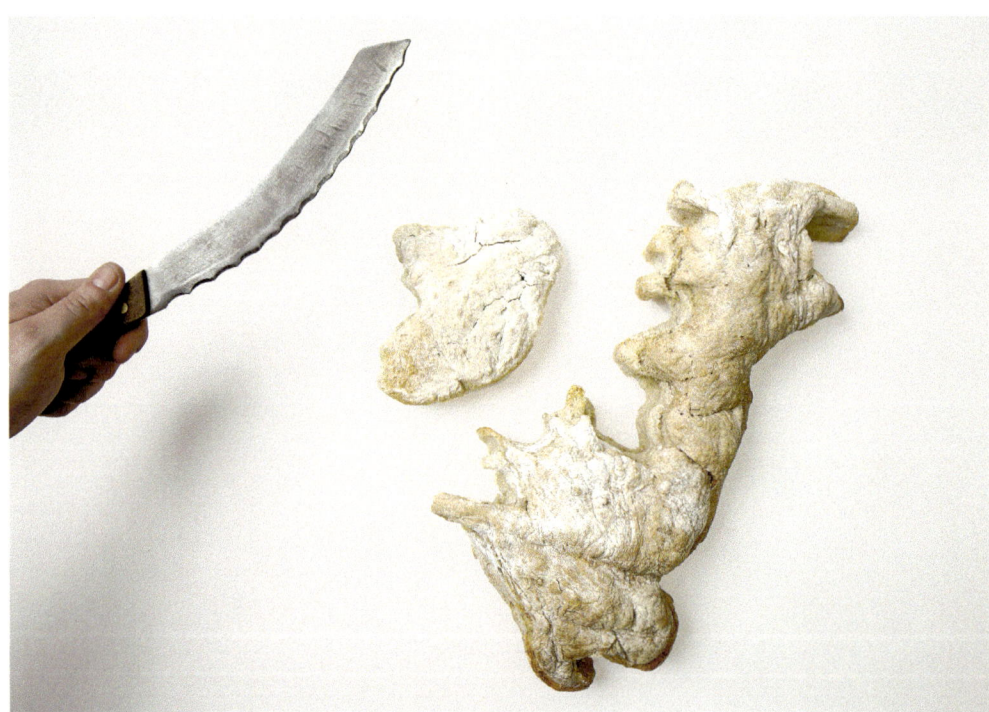

Immaterial technologies

Technologies used in the production of gaming environments, internet platforms and virtual and augmented realities offer much potential and many opportunities for illustration. There are clear commonalities in the behaviours and strategies used to engage audiences such as the use of character, narrative and subjective experience. Appropriating the systems and properties operating within these environments (i.e. strategic interaction, interface navigation, etc), could see illustration become adaptive to interaction, stripped entirely of material substance, existing as an encounter within a wholly immaterial environment and/or as intangible artefacts within real world settings. Works that function with use of the personal technologies that pervade everyday living – smartphones, tablets, computers – also broaden the reach for engagement.

SHHH!
TATE BRITAIN
Jack Sachs

In this short film, the viewer encounters illustrator and animator, Jack Sachs' CG characters inhabiting the Tate Britain. The walk-through format mimics a first-person gaming experience, with the intention that the viewer feels as if they are gliding through the gallery space happening upon these surreal vignettes. Using motion-capture technology (the setting is real, HD footage was taken in the gallery and will be a familiar setting to many) Sachs is able to situate his digitally crafted illustrations in the 'real world', albeit through the medium of animation.

4 CRAFTING

Immaterial technologies

SHHH!
TATE BRITAIN
Jack Sachs

AT SOME POINT, THIS TREE WILL FALL
Jack Wild

A strange, solitary organism, redolent of a giant dandelion, sways in a whirring wind, so vivid you brace for the chill to hit your skin. A flock of crude, birdlike figures ebb and flow, continuously circling the plantlike structure. The motion of the atmosphere causes seeds, or perhaps leaves, to disperse. They are caught in the air currents until they inevitably fall, disappearing as if absorbed into the glowing red soil. The only other sign of life is a singular signpost with a notice nailed to it. The message scrawled in red lettering reads *at some point this tree will fall*. This landscape is other-worldly and nameless. It cannot be visited but is accessible at all hours through the lens of a screen; the movement of the cursor allowing the viewer to position and control their gaze.

This is a landscape without physicality, yet it is not imaginary and there is a creator. The digital designer, Jack Wild, has developed a virtual environment that exists entirely within its own real time. The atmosphere is not governed by nature but by the semi-random algorithm, Perlin noise. The title of the work references the fact that the seemingly organic structure will eventually collapse in response to the virtual weather system, only it can't because it doesn't *really* exist. However, Wild stresses the sensations the work provokes are real: the curiosity and the anticipation of waiting for the inevitable to occur. The experience is governed by the tension of waiting for an event that may happen at any given moment.

Although this is an indeterminable environment, there are several parallels with the tangible world. The framing of the screen, the only means through which the work can be viewed, easily translates metaphorically as a window one might gaze out of onto a natural scene. The screen-reliant interaction and constant availability bears resemblance to how global current affairs are encountered; situations we know or believe to be real and current, stir emotion in the absence of any tangible experience. While this work can be experienced anywhere, all that is required is an internet accessible device with a screen. However, the knowing participation of the audience is vital in consolidating it as a work of visual communication. *At Some Point, This Tree Will Fall* describes a narrative screen, an articulation of an idea that provokes a response while communicating several messages. Here, the virtual serving as a way to provide authentic sensation. It is Wild who poses the question: *I don't see why this is not illustration?*

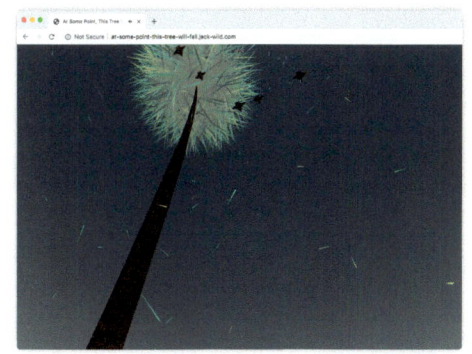

5 ACTIVISM

138 — Am I political?
— Power play
139 — An informed practice
— The visual identity of protest
140 — Détournement
— The illustrator's joke
143 — Who do you think I am?
147 — The meme
148 — Future visions
152 — Illustration as event
156 — Models of behaviour
158 — 'How can I help you?'

TO BE
AN
ACTIVIST
IS TO POSE A CHALLENGE,
OFFER A COUNTER ARGUMENT
OR EXPRESS RESISTANCE AGAINST
A MAINSTREAM AUTHORITY
OR
ACCEPTED NORM.

Am I political?

Politics is a complex principle with multiple connotations. The use of the term is often understood as relating to party politics; the forming of cohorts that represent the views of others in order to govern a particular state, country or body of people. More generally, politics can be understood as the structures, systems and negotiations through which people exist and live among one another. This can also be understood in terms more immediately relatable, such as how institutions like schools and hospitals are managed; how assets are divided within a company, and even the hierarchies of power within a family home. Being engaged in politics doesn't only refer to an understanding of government legislative design; political dynamics are omnipresent and operating constantly within all aspects of everyday life.

The feminist slogan, 'The personal is political', popularised in the late 1960s by Carol Hanisch, describes how everyday experiences are inextricably connected to larger political and social structures. 'The personal is political' was first used to encourage women to relate their personal experiences to pervading power structures, now it is more widely applied to advocate personal experience as a site for political analysis – a contemporary example being the Everyday Sexism Project, a global online catalogue of instances of sexism encountered on a daily basis. While the languages and knowledge frequently employed within global political debate can appear exclusionary, direct engagement with these discussions can stem from examining issues and events closer to home.

Power play

In the broadest sense, activism is described as a concerted effort to incite change, facilitate engagement or voice opinion. The influence of 'activisation' may be physical, intellectual and/or emotional. To be an activist is to pose a challenge, offer a counter argument or express resistance against a mainstream authority or accepted norm. In this regard, activism calls for a redistribution of power and an expression of alternative voices and opinions. How a creative skill set is best applied with these intentions will be first determined by gaining an in-depth knowledge of the supported cause. This will allow for a better understanding of the issues and injustices at play, and help to pinpoint the best ways they can be addressed.

Research often begins through familiarisation of the historical contexts of the plight, as well as current circumstances. Even within a historical case there are likely to be relationships or themes relevant to contemporary affairs at local, national or global level. Understanding the various positions and opinions held within debates will allow for more detailed insight and can help form a more convincing argument. While researching, continually reflect on what action, influence or change is desired and how best this might be achieved with the immediate means available. Establishing a case-specific knowledge will allow a more refined understanding of where the power inequalities within the area of concern lie. This can then be examined within a wider theoretical framework of how power is exerted and utilised. There are various schools of philosophical and critical thought as to how power operates and how it is yielded within society. Karl Marx, Michel

Foucault, and Guy Debord are often cited as key theorists relevant within the field of visual communication, and are considered to be forerunners to much contemporary critical thinking regarding social activism. Gaining a general understanding of the key concepts provides a theoretical lens through which to examine the subject of concern. Political dynamics are complex, and it will be likely that multiple discriminations and tensions will be operating. The oppression might be intersectional with the discrimination being the result of several interconnected prejudices. Research into critical debate can be tailored accordingly to gain a more nuanced understanding, for example, it may become apparent that a singular study might require knowledge of feminism, Marxism and queer theory. While a total revolution within an individual project is unlikely, an understanding of the power dynamics will help determine what creative strategies will be best to help support change and enable social justice. Establishing a contextual, historical and theoretical grounding will provide a richer comprehension of the subject matter, which will directly inform creative making through allowing considered decisions to be made.

An informed practice

As a mediated art form, illustration is often reproduced and is context specific. The situating of the work, the locations where it is encountered, as well as the circumstances within which it is experienced and by whom, will all influence how the work communicates. A creative practice that voices subversive or critical ideas has the potential to be compromised by all of these factors. An illustration practice never operates in total isolation. The work is created within certain economic and social conditions and might be facilitated by institutions, companies, funding bodies or private individuals. The various agendas of all concerned parties may not always fully align within the intentions of an illustrator, and it will be necessary to contemplate how these associations will impact upon the intentions of the work. Compromises might have the potential to both hinder and aid the success of the work; for example, taking advantage of an offer of corporate distribution could allow your work to reach mass audiences that would be otherwise hard to access. Professional associations and relationships can have lingering impacts; it is important to deliberate the potential long-term and short-term pros and cons.

The visual identity of protest

Graphic imagery is often the instinctive means of communicating when needing to voice opinion or concern with economy of means, clarity and urgency. Protest and activist movements throughout history are often recognised through association with distinctive visual identities. The aesthetics, forms and strategies for engagement will be informed by a number of factors. These will include the technologies of the time; the available means of production; the expertise, experience and/or identities of producing the visual content and the particular concerns within the struggle or conflict. Appropriating the aesthetic of a well-established protest movement can form an immediately recognisable alignment between a contemporary activist artwork and a historical cause. A graphic image, through continual reuse, may also go on to transcend its original

---

Marxism

A body of thought based on the political and economic theories of Karl Marx (1818–1883) and Friedrich Engels (1820–1895) consisting of two core interrelated concepts: a critique of the capitalist economy and the summation that the history of all societies can be understood as a class struggle between the proletariat (the working class) and the bourgeoisie (the ruling class).

Michel Foucault (1926–1984)

Historian and philosopher interested in how knowledge functions as a form of power, particularly by examining the history of dominant institutions within society, such as hospitals, prisons and psychiatric care facilities, and agreed definitions of illness, mental health and sexuality.

context and meaning. For example the logo created by Gerald Holtom for the British Campaign for Nuclear Disarmament, intentionally never copyrighted to promote freedom of use, is now internationally understood as denoting peace. Holtom's logo is now so distinctive that any reference to its graphic visual form, even if highly adapted, spark immediate recognition, serving to associate the imagery with promoting peaceful protest. Relying on visual associations to communicate requires the audience to have some pre-existing knowledge to comprehend the meaning of your work. The placement and contexts of the illustrative work, as well as an understanding of the target audience's likely experience and knowledge, will help support decisions as to how to present information, so intended associations are clear and easily understood.

The appropriation of a familiar visual aesthetic may be an efficient strategy to engage and communicate, but it is also important to fully understand the rationales for using such a method, and to ensure that it is not a strategy used due to a lack of imagination or ingenuity. Consider the relevance of the creative techniques used in the creation and dissemination of the work. Often, the means of production holds agency with the audience as well as the cause and is ultimately dictated by the resources available to the illustrator. For example, second wave feminist zines were created using technologies and processes that were accessible and affordable to those working within the movement; paste paper collage, photocopying and handmade publications. In translating this to a contemporary practice, the intent may be to evoke the sense of a subversive print culture, but it also begs questioning if whether mimicking the methods relevant to the specific conditions of a historic cause is an appropriate way of engaging audiences in a contemporary debate.

Détournement

Contemporary life is image-saturated. Mass media, advertising and popular culture pervade and influence all aspects of everyday life. Overexposure can lead to complacency and a lack of critical consideration of the manipulative content conveyed in these messages. The creative *détournement* of popular visual material can serve to alert audiences through representing the very same content, but in such a way that prompts a rereading that is contradictory to the original agenda. Collage or montage is commonly associated with this creative practice, whereby new images are formed through manipulating the actual visual content produced by the entity being critiqued. In such works it is not only the content of the imagery that communicates; texture, materiality and formatting can also inflect meaning and resonate with particular historical sociopolitical and cultural associations. Reappropriating or repurposing familiar propagandist imagery can also challenge power dynamics through subverting their original intentions.

The illustrator's joke

Comedy is a familiar strategy used by illustrators to voice political critique. Comic timing in static imagery requires much skill and crafting. Humorous images may operate with immediate effect through a single image, whereby all elements communicate instantaneously or within a very short period of time. For this to be successful, the audience is required to have some prior awareness of the information referenced. The imagery used must be explicit so as to trigger a prompt recognition; being too cryptic or using visual codes that need time to be deciphered will delay comprehension, risking the 'punch-line' being lost. This is particularly pertinent when the illustration has a limited time to engage audiences, for example, when being glanced at in a newspaper or during a street protest. Conversely, the humor in operating within an illustration may need time for reflection with full understanding arrived at after a controlled delay of information. This can be achieved through sequencing – several images operating together to create a narrative situation during which tension is controlled, leading to climactic resolve.

Humour is a powerful tool that can encourage both inclusivity and exclusivity. Comedy can engage and unite people through mutual understanding and a shared agreement with the comment or analysis. Be it intentional or not, humour can also exclude and isolate individuals, particularly when references are used that cannot be readily understood by all. Found in both mainstream and counterculture media platforms, satirical illustration humour is well established as a method to voice political critique. Satirical comedy often includes the use of mimicry, irony and ridicule, and can be hugely influential in undermining powerful authoritarian individuals and institutes. Familiar approaches include representations of eminent public figures with exaggerated physical characterisations and/or portrayals of topical debates and events through sometimes fantastical visual parodies.

Not only the remit of the professional illustrator, satirical imagery featured heavily in the protest banners produced for the 2017 Women's March, the major target of critique being Donald Trump, the president of the United States of America at the time. The Women's March drew together numbers in the tens of thousands and saw a vast display of banners using highly creative text and image compositions, many of which communicated using imagery alone. More generally, protest marches and demonstrations are particularly unique events where professional and vernacular examples of what could be understood as illustrative imagery are presented together to communicate with equal visual impact, without a sense of hierarchy. The Women's March evidenced that humourous, creative imagery is an instinctive method to express a succinct and impactful opinion, regardless of formal artistic training.

WOMEN'S MARCH,
LONDON, 2017

The protest is where the accessibility of illustration is most eloquently demonstrated; professional and vernacular uses of the medium are presented and communicate together with equal impact.

Intersectionality

The instance of multiple forms of discrimination, i.e. gender, sexuality, disability, race, age, being in operation simultaneously.

Queerness

A challenge to heteronormative societal establishments and ideologies. Queerness is often associated with same sex desire as well as gender and identity politics. Queer theory is a field of critical inquiry concerned with the theorising of queerness, as well as offering queer readings and assessment of texts and cultural phenomena. Philosopher Judith Butler (b. 1956) is a key proponent of the movement.

5 ACTIVISM

The illustrator's joke

WOMEN'S MARCH,
LONDON, 2017

Who do you think I am?

Illustration can be used to address debates surrounding identity politics. Illustrators can create new representations of cultures, social groups and people that allow for alternative narratives and viewpoints to be understood. Such works may operate by offering new visualisations that challenge dominant portrayals, confront stereotypes or reveal insights into seemingly exclusive or enigmatic communities.

Graphic, heavily lined and uncompromising, Olivia Twist uses thick-tipped marker pens to create her suitably bold character studies. Her images are recognisable as portraiture in the traditional sense, only within Twist's illustrations, the subjects are people of colour, often youthful Black British people caught in the throes of contemporary urban life. Often composed to meet the eye of the viewer, the images vividly convey a sense personality through careful attention to physical gestures, posture and the detailing of cultural indicators such clothing, fashions, hairstyling and jewellery. Figures are captured in situ, living in the everyday. We meet individuals mid conversation, find them eating in fast-food restaurants or en route to Sunday worship. The scenes are portrayed from the viewpoint of a personal encounter, these are people who are well known: friends and family, even Twist's own image slips into her compositions. There are also those who are not intimate acquaintances but are nonetheless familiar presences: the neighbours on the housing estate or the rowdy school children at the back of the bus, who Twist admits she would have been among at one time. Twist is highly perceptive in representing the locations of both informal and formal gatherings and the various groups that frequent them. For example, the chicken shop and the domestic family kitchen are both environments within which a cultural milieu is present, with its own distinctive codes of conduct and systems of communication. As one of Twist's eavesdropping text pieces declares: 'I know one too many people who don't know how to finish their wings properly.'

The sense of the familiar and ordinary are key tenets; the attention to details within the mundanity of lived experience that when extrapolated and represented, command attention and recognition. Twist describes this as the 'shock of the familiar' within her illustration. The illustrations draw out details or situations that are commonplace within a personal experience, or aligned to a cultural or subcultural identity but are usually tacit and unrecorded. The images prompt a sense of affiliation and belonging among the groups they depict, through formalising and recognising rituals and cultural habits. These illustrations also consciously allow those on the outside a view in, with a sensitivity to the fact that what is a social norm to one group can seem entirely alien to another.

Feminism
Broad grouping of international and historically specific ideologies addressing the oppressions, rights and interests of women. Many branches of feminism exist and coexist with varying concerns and emphasises.

Non-binary gender
Individuals who reject being identified according to conventional male or female gender definitions.

Propaganda
Images, information, ideas or opinions that lack objectivity, with the intent to incite particular emotional responses, sell ideas or goods, further political agenda or promote particular ideologies or causes.

Capitalism
An economic system characterised by the production of commodities, private ownership and control of property, business and industry for profit.

3.45
Olivia Twist

1: YOU PAID FOURTEEN QUID FOR YOUR TRIM? TANVIR, YOU GOT RIPPED OFF MAN.

TANVIR: BRO, HE WASHED IT TOO. THIS ISNT JUST A BASIC TRIM. LOOK AT THE PRECSION!

Say it with your chest sis

5 ACTIVISM

Who do you think I am?

3.45
Olivia Twist

**ME, MY MUM AND MY NAN HAVE BEEN ON A DIET SINCE JANUARY. MY NAN IS LOOSING THE MOST WEIGHT THOUGH, ME AND MUM ARE WELL JEAL!
I MEAN WHAT IS THE POINT OF P.E?**

The meme

The visual meme draws together text and image to create meaning in ways similar to conventional forms of illustration. In essence, the meme is an isolated narrative that operates through creating comedic visual situations that reference familiar cultural icons, ideas and behaviours. Often, these text-image juxtapositions converge aspects of culture that are considered contradictory or contentious, but their alignment actually serves to reinforce the desired message. The comedy, a result of the tension created through this creative repositioning, is often akin to satire. Easily produced and without any direct financial costs, the crafting of a meme is not concerned with the production of a beautiful composition. Rather the ingenuity lies in how the source material is manipulated to create new meaning. Often, images from popular culture are used to ensure memes are instantaneously understood and require very little intellectual investment, planning or self-awareness on the part of the audience.

The meme is also distinctive in that it is entirely dependent on the internet, existing primarily within social media networks. The meme is at once the content of a message and a means of distribution. The creators are often unknown, as memes operate through being continually adapted to be made relevant to different topics as they travel through the internet.

Memes are shared for a range of intentions: to relate a feeling, make someone laugh or to share solidarity. Often, the subject matter describes a mundane everyday experience, which is then re-contextualised to comment on initially seemingly unrelated aspects of life, such as popular culture, current affairs, social policy, political figures, etc.

The ease with which memes are shared and their ability to engage audiences en masse make them a powerful tool through which to communicate, allowing messages to be distributed swiftly and succinctly. A meme that is unsuccessful ceases to exist, as the means of distribution is entirely reliant on the viewer sharing them within their own social media networks. Embedding themselves within online platforms that might be accessed during both professional and personal time, the meme is able to attract those not intending or expecting to engage in dialogues relating to sociopolitical issues. The meme, therefore, is potentially a device that could be used for strategic creative activism, but there are factors to be aware of. Once a meme enters the ether, the creator loses control over content and aesthetics. The original meaning may be lost through alterations, or be subverted to communicate messages you do not wish to align with. Relinquishing authorship may not be appropriate if you want the meme to be recognised as an artwork attributed to you.

Anonymity can also imply a mitigation of responsibility. How well an opinion or message is supported can be determined by how long it continues to propagate. However, the meme offers no space for dialogue, in essence it is a one-directional form of communication – a powerful tool, one where no retort is possible. In terms of inciting activism, sharing can evidence support, but this does not directly equate to informing direct social change. The specific context of social media as a platform for disseminating ideas also makes your messages vulnerable to being trapped within echo chambers, only heard and shared among your own community, who essentially already share the same beliefs.

Future visions

Illustrators have the ability to visualise the future. Depicting an alternative reality, whether hopeful or cautionary, enables others to conceive and desire a future outside of what is known. The aim of such works is to understand the concerns, fears or preoccupations of today and imagine possible resolutions or worst-case scenarios. A visual description or illustrated narrative is not the actualisation of radical change, but it can serve to make tangible a view outside of the situation we currently inhabit. This can then become a powerful catalyst for political radicalisation. Speculative futures are created with the intention of being purely hypothetical. There does not need to be a dramatic change in order to draw attention to social injustice, systemic inequalities or environmental change.

Depicting a continuation of the current reality, or an exaggeration of policy or of a natural phenomenon highlights what might be 'round the corner' and is exemplified in Cat Sims' short comic, 'Black Matter'. Part zombie apocalypse, part psychogeographic wandering, this hybrid narrative about a young woman's journey to a hastily arranged online date, is set in a world eerily familiar and yet unreal. Contemporary issues, such as loneliness and isolation, mental health issues, designer drugs and gentrification, are envisioned through the lens of a 'not-too-distant future'. Set in a cityscape plagued by social inequality; graffiti and abandoned desolate buildings sit adjacent to private luxury developments; tropical palm trees growing in a recognisably London setting are a nod towards the inevitable results of climate change.

Sims' narrative forces the audience to see a current reality through a filter that illuminates a future that may not be too far away. Here, speculative fiction can allow radical change to occur within a fantastical domain where potential social scenarios are realised and analysed from a position of safety. Imaginative renderings of 'what might be' need not be entirely fantastical. Fictional futures may draw influence from past historic events extending what is known about human social relations and responses, and applying them to more extreme circumstances.

BLACK MATTER
Cat Sims

Utopia

A vision or concept of an ideal society or environment, which can be imaged but never realised in actuality.

ACTIVISM
Future visions

BLACK MATTER
Cat Sims

BLACK MATTER
Cat Sims

Illustration as event

The illustrator may feel it necessary to create a situation or event that is dependent on audience participation as part of their creative practice. The 'situation' referred to here is not a strategy separate from the creative work, used to draw interest and engage audiences as, for example, a private viewing of an exhibition. Rather the work of illustration manifests through a happening that takes place in real time. In such cases the work of illustration is not confined to being understood as an image-based outcome but as a time specific event. The illustration as event may be realised in a number of ways, for example: a protest, a workshop or a performance, as appropriate to the intentions of the project. An illustrative work encompassing a live event challenges the audience/illustration dynamic.

Rather than encountering an illustrative artefact post-production, the audience engages with the work as it unfolds in real time and they may become complicit in the performance of the work. The illustration as event also challenges the position of the illustrator as image maker. The creative role occupied may be more akin to that of a facilitator, performer or curator. While this concept introduces the notion that an illustration may not need to have a physical manifestation, it is not to suggest that the physical image or artefact is entirely absent. The illustration event is fixed in time, but its legacy and image may endure through recording or documentation.

GREEN BELT PROPERTIES: COSTING A HOUSE
Jon Halls

Sections of Hayes Common within the London Borough of Bromley have been physically cordoned off with vivid blue industrial rope. Within the threshold, a simply-designed but distinctively corporate 'For Sale' placard has been thrust into the earth. Standing in red and white, the message is bold against the dense green of the woodland. Resonant of both the protest demonstration placard as well as estate agent signage, the information provided is concise: the land is for sale through the provocatively-named developer Green Belt Properties. A situation in real time has been created. Green Belt Properties is a fiction, but at the moment of encounter this is not yet known.

This situation is one of a series of what illustrator activist Jon Halls describes as 'interventions' addressing the effects of human progress and development on the environment. Halls devised Green Belt Properties as a way of engaging seemingly disparate social groups to consider wider environmental issues by placing the threat 'closer to home'. For Halls, who was raised in the area, Hayes Common is home and holds much personal significance to the environmentalist as an invaluable green space within the urban residential environment. In order to gain understanding of the significance and uses of the woodland beyond his own personal experience, Halls sought out and met with various volunteer groups, as well as local council workers and heritage sector organisations.

Recognising the diversity of usage of the common land in contemporary life, Halls employs a variety of activist strategies to engage multiple and seemingly disparate social groups. The physical partitioning of land creates an event, a rupture to the norm. A simple act, but powerfully symbolic, a physical threat is created to a landscape, which by heritage is an entitlement to the everyman. This human 'intervention' made by the activist does not dictate a response, but offers the means to investigate further by visiting a website constructed by Halls.

Halls further uses these defined areas of woodland for close intimate study through drawing, which the illustrator also recognises as a form of activism. The rendering of these images through the physical act of making allows time for contemplation of the landscape. The drawings are an activation; redolent of the environment they address, but within the imagery, various ecosystems and habitats are emphasised beyond what might be immediately obvious to human users of the land. The results form a visual survey, illuminating what is unseen or disregarded, magnifying the potential for loss. This is not a vision of a speculative future but a celebration, and a call for protection of what is already present.

The website www.greenbeltproperties.co.uk (no longer accessible), then, becomes a conduit presenting the various forms of knowledge collected and curated by Halls about the common. Pictorial illustrations, personal and critical writing all inform the user of the intentions of the project. The information serves to engage and inform, articulating key facts as well affirming the historical context of the common land. Several wider issues are made pertinent within this one specific location, such as littering and physical fragmentation of land for pathways. We are encouraged to contemplate the impact of what we deem are our needs on the landscape.

Halls also offers potential solutions taken from successful historical strategies; these seem unfeasible, even ludicrous, within contemporary society – the reintegration of livestock onto the land is one such example. A forum is also available for users to enter into dialogue about the presented ideas. In the absence of answers, the intention here is to create a conversation and foster a community for those already bound together through their mutual use of this common land.

Neoliberalism

A political ideology and economic system that values and promotes free trade, deregulation of economic markets and private entrepreneurship with an accompanying ideology of individualism.

Relational aesthetics

Term offered by Nicolas Bourriaud (b. 1965) to describe works of art that perform through participatory involvement with audiences, often in social contexts and environments rather than in a gallery setting. Critic Claire Bishop (b. 1971) challenges the ambitions of participatory art and the criteria by which it is judged, positing that a lack of aesthetic criticism has meant that these works are judged on ethical or political terms rather than by artistic or aesthetic standards.

ACTIVISM

Illustration as event

GREEN BELT PROPERTIES: COSTING A HOUSE
Jon Halls

Images are screen grabs from the website www.greenbeltproperties.co.uk, taken at time of printing.

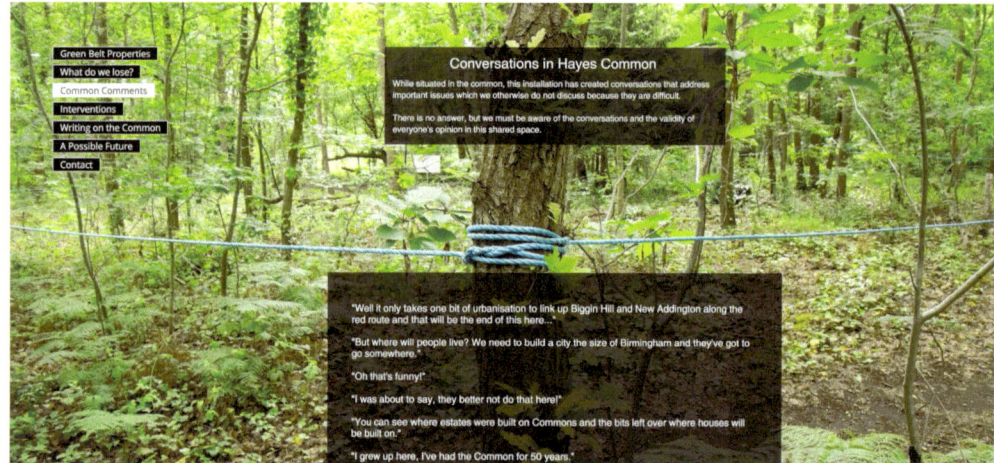

Recuperation

Capitalism's ability to absorb and neutralise critique and then represent it with the means to suit its own agenda.

Models of behaviour

When using an illustrative practice to reach out and engage audiences in conversation or critical debate, it may be helpful to investigate the communal spaces already being utilised within that specific community. Consider what the informal or formal customs or circumstances are that draw together the people you are trying to engage, for example, this may be the sharing of a meal, a weekly sports activity or a discussion group. Using models of social activities that are familiar to your identified group may help to encourage participation and help foster conversations more naturally. The subject matters addressed may be serious, or even grave, but that need not mean inspiration can't be drawn from the moments of relief or respite that are already successfully uniting people.

THE CURIOUS CASE
OF MAVIS DAVIS
Rebecca Davies

A shock of auburn tresses is teased sky-high in a firmly set beehive. Heavily powered eyelids peer out to meeting your gaze from behind a pair of wide-frame spectacles. Glossed ruby lips pursed ready for banter. This is Mavis Davis, adorned with hoop earrings and synthetic fabrics, she is the quick-witted, uncompromising proprietress of The Oasis Social Club, the public house that places the emphasis on 'public'. 'Donna Plagg', the Hull landlady, is just one of the many personas inhabited by Rebecca Davies, whose practice as a creative activist uses performative events that reference familiar social customs and rituals of gathering.

Following the model of the local institutions, such as the community hall and the pub, The Oasis Social Club appears as a drawn-to-scale illustration of a public house brought to life, complete with suitably patterned flooring and tinsel curtains. A portable venue, the club has made appearances in numerous locations such as Preston, Hull and Stoke, all post-industrial towns striving to sustain regeneration in the north of England. The events, hosted by Davies, usually in character, and the team who work with her, are creative adaptations of activities customary within any social club, such as bingo, karaoke and aerobics classes. While delivered with humour and a celebratory sense of occasion, underlying the activities are topics of urgent and serious concern with in the immediate locale. Davies' projects are often informed in response to national and local government legislations, specifically those addressing social welfare, housing and urban redevelopment, and how the impact of such measures are felt by localised communities. Rather than being interpretations, Davies' exaggerated charismatic personas are amalgamations of real people, known and observed, and are archetypes recognisable in some form in all communities. Through embodying these illustrated characters, Davies acts as a mouthpiece through which to debate topical concerns and communicate opinions and experiences specific to that character identity. Using this voice, Davies articulates perspectives that are not always projected outside of specific community circles.

Davies' practice is never a sole endeavour. The projects are produced with the help of creative collaborators and liaison between arts organisations and local government, to support communities to determine, deliver and achieve goals that are realistic and sustainable. The activism at play within Rebecca Davies' practice is imbedded within her life and the political within the everyday. Whether it be touring the United Kingdom in an ice cream van to collect oral histories or relocating to Stoke-on-Trent to facilitate the rejuvenation of a disused pub as a community-led arts space,

Davies situates herself within the environment, working from the group as an invested citizen bridging distances and flattening hierarchies between facilitator and participants, and authority and autonomy.

Socially engaged practice

Works of art or design that involve communities in action or debate, to raise awareness or improve their local environment. Often, it is associated with activism because it provides an arena for people to have agency in their own lives, and is often politically motivated.

ACTIVISM

Models of behaviour

THE CURIOUS CASE OF MAVIS DAVIS
Rebecca Davies

'How can I help you?'

There are ways that illustrators can employ their skills outside of guerrilla or self-initiated projects to support social justice. Rather than establishing an entirely new movement, it may be more impactful to approach an existing organisation and simply ask how your expertise can be of use. Acknowledgement of a specific illustrative practice and training will have limitations, but there are valuable skills that can be contributed within a wider task force. Exchanging knowledge with others who have different expertise will extend experience and help determine how best to contribute as an illustrator. When working within diverse teams be mindful of agendas and/or opinions regarding creative solutions, as these may very likely differ. What might appear from the perspective of the illustrator as conceptually sound or appropriate might not be recognised as such by all. In such circumstances it is worth considering what the higher shared goals of the project are, who the ideal beneficiaries are, and whether creative integrity is worth the compromise.

THE VISUAL IMAGINARY
Luise Vormittag

 The sociopolitically engaged designer, writer and educator Luise Vormittag has been using her practice as a visual communicator to work with the London-based charitable organisation Latin Elephant. The charity was formed to support the long established Latin American and other minority ethnic migrant community in the Elephant and Castle area of South London, who have been threatened by

Guy Debord
(1931-1994)

Philosopher Guy Debord penned *The Society of the Spectacle* (1967), which analyses how consumer driven capitalism supersedes all other forms of social control, like poverty or religion; dissenters are pacified through consumption and individuals are isolated. Debord's theory of 'the commodity spectacle' describes all social relationships as being mediated by images, and a real or authentic society is replaced by mere representation. Debord's ideas can be read as prescient of twenty-first century phenomena like celebrity culture, information technologies and neoliberalism.

Détournement

A revision or reworking of a past motif or media so as to have the opposite meaning or message.

a vast urban regeneration development. Vormittag began to work with the charity in their mission to defend the small traders working in and around the iconic Elephant and Castle Shopping Centre, soon to be lost within the development works. Considering the relocation strategy proposals submitted by the developers to the council to be inadequate, the charity wanted to acquire evidence of the importance of the traders within the community and the potential impact of their loss within the multi-ethnic area. Vormittag explains how the visual appearance of the Elephant and Castle area with its ailing facade seemingly supports the argument to demolish, rebuild and regenerate. When constructing a convincing counter argument as to why these places are of sociocultural significance and should be conserved, photography fails, as what is captured is a record of the aesthetically questionable surface appearance. It is the memories of the lives lived in that place; the stories of people who are integrated and invested in the area that must be communicated. Vormittag describes this as the 'topographical imaginary': the mental image that is held of a place and the contrast between this vision of lived experience and that which is seen with the naked eye of an outsider. Considering this, Vormittag's concern was how to graphically represent a social dynamic that is certainly present, but not immediately visible. People inscribe themselves through their stories into a location, how then can that imaginary image be articulated?

Vormittag devised a workshop, which she held a number of times in and around the Shopping Centre. She sketched out a large-format map that roughly charted the area; the emphasis was not on exact cartographic measurements but to create a framework. People within the local community, both Latin Americans and anybody else who uses the Shopping Centre, were invited to write and draw directly onto the maps, detailing their favourite places or their most frequently travelled routes. The intention was not so much to chart different ways of navigating the area, but rather to gently encourage dialogue regarding the locations that were most poignant to people and why. Vormittag found the strategy of asking about a familiar journey was a more fruitful way to prompt conversations that led to more meaningful memories. Contained within these collaborative maps are multiple histories and narratives from which alternative landmarks, or 'castles', emerged, such as favourite bars, shops or meeting places. The maps then also serve as form of data collection that share a vision of an urban landscape known by this distinctive community.

5 ACTIVISM

'How can I help you?'

THE VISUAL IMAGINARY
Luise Vormittag

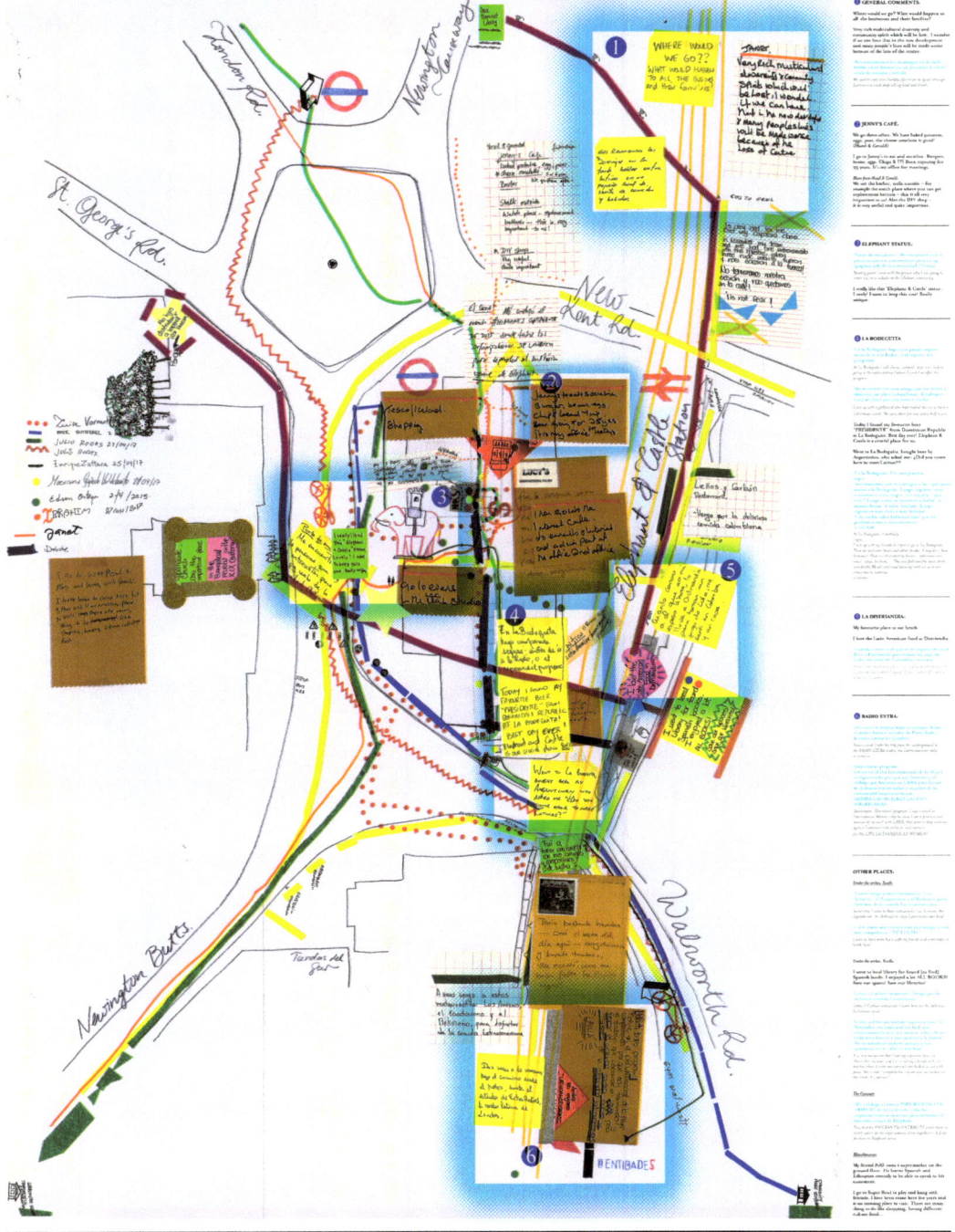

ACTIVISM

'How can I help you?'

SHY RADICALS:
THE ANTISYSTEMIC POLITICS
OF THE MILITANT INTROVERT
Hamja Ahsan (Author) and
Rose Nordin (Illustrator)

Shy Radicals: The Antisystemic Politics of the Militant Introvert is a compact and discreet little book. Perfect bound with soft cover and flush edges, it is simple in form, fits neatly into the hand and is equally comfortably tucked into a back pocket.

Contained within this tidy volume are a series of comprehensive texts articulating the demands of a newly formed political party: The Shy Radicals. United in mutual animosity, the quiet, introverted and socially awkward have mobilised; a revolution has been imagined. Their mandate is to rise against the recognised enemy: the 'extrovert supremacists'. A work of speculative fiction, the carefully observed narrative reflects personal experiences and knowledge of the multifaceted arts practitioner, curator and activist Hamja Ahsan.

Ahsan's social observations astutely articulate the perspective of a marginal population seldom represented as a distinct group: the introverts. Ahsan recognised and felt victim to a form of discrimination for which there was no existing liberation movement, and so devised an entirely new ideology. The writing is effortlessly littered with witty neologisms and wordplay; we are introduced to the constitution of the speculative homeland the 'Shy People's Republic of Aspergistan' governed by the 'Shyria Law' legislative system. National defence is enforced by 'Armed Isolationists' and 'Trendy Club' is used as a catch-all term describing all congregations displaying behaviour deemed offensive by the radicals.

The mobilisation here may not be immediately visible, but the text serves to attribute an identity for a neglected marginal population. Not only does the content of the writing champion gentleness and introversion, but the very act of reading offers a sense of solace and inclusion. Here the use of a fictional yet relatable narrative fosters a sense of belonging and togetherness without any overt physical action or grouping of people.

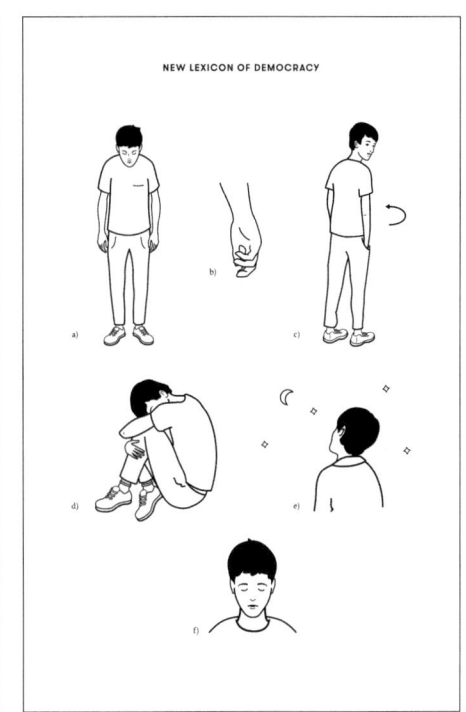

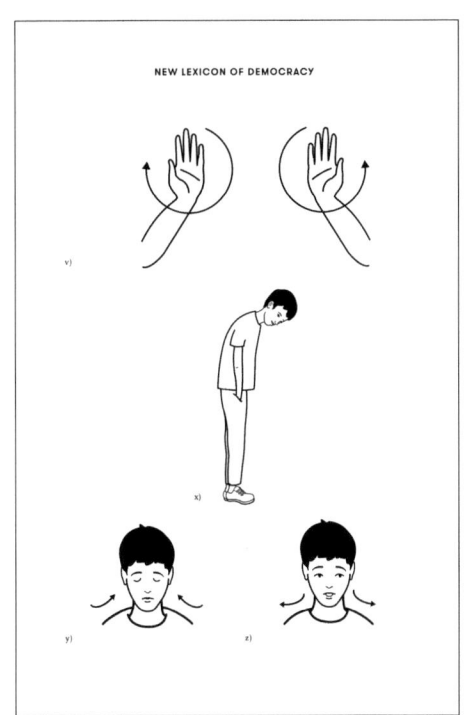

Consciousness raising

Feminist form of activism, where small, women-only groups discuss and share their personal experiences with the intention of understanding individual experiences as collective ones that are the result of living in a patriarchal society and as such are not the responsibility of the individual.

Alienation

Concept devised by Karl Marx (1818-1883) to describe the exclusory, separating and dehumanising effect that capitalism, and more specifically, nineteenth-century industrialised production, had on workers. Long hours, mass production lines and poor wages alienated workers from each other, their work and the goods they produced.

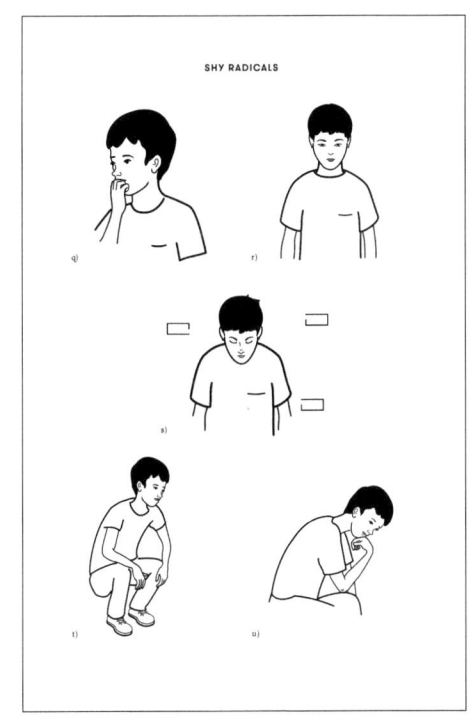

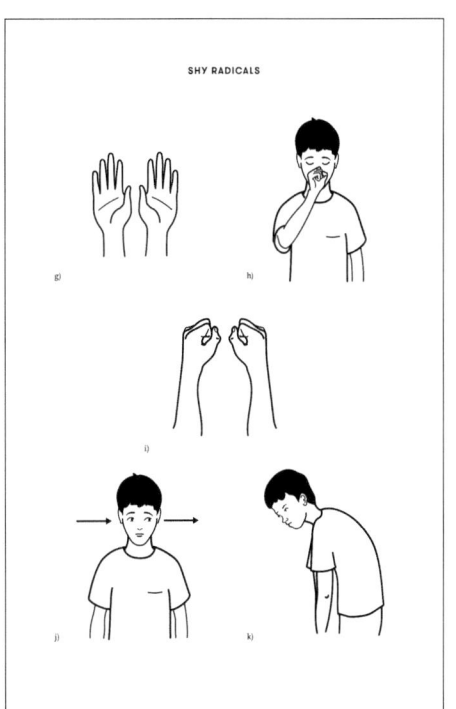

6 EDUCATION

166 — What is your philosophy?
167 — What is an education space?
      — Signature pedagogies
173 — Shop talk
176 — Learning *through* illustration
178 — Residency as method
181 — Documents of experience
186 — Illustration-based research
189 — Data visualisation
193 — The language of reliability
197 — Interactive illustration

FACILITATING LEARNING
INVOLVES CREATING SITUATIONS,
CONSTRUCTING TOOLS
AND DEVELOPING METHODS
WHICH AID THE ACQUISITION
OF KNOWLEDGE.

What is your philosophy?

Those wanting to incorporate education into an illustration practice should consider the different roles the illustrator-educator can adopt, the various dynamics in operation during the process of learning, and the intentions of the knowledge being gained. To educate is to tell, explain, interpret, suggest, facilitate, expose, test, make connections, develop or understand. Facilitating learning involves creating situations, constructing tools and developing methods which aid the acquisition of knowledge. Learning is not necessarily dependent on specific training nor associated with particular institutions. While there are periods of time during which learning is intensified, such as when in formal education, learning is in fact an ongoing and lifelong activity. It occurs at all ages and is not restricted to a particular setting. The home, workplace, playground and urban or natural environments can all be educational spaces.

Numerous pedagogic philosophies have been developed and contested throughout history, from Platonic thought which prescribed that social justice can be achieved through equal opportunities to education, to constructivist learning where learners construct their own personal and individual knowledge as they learn, by making their own discoveries. More recently, educational theorists have critically addressed the value of play, curiosity, social interaction, work experience and direct experiences with the environment. Such ideas are of particular interest to illustrators, who frequently work outside of conventional learning environments and institutions. Within an illustrator's practice, dialogic approaches and collaborative learning may feel particularly relevant, with the view that we educate for reasons of emancipation, individuality or self-expression. Alternatively, the belief might be held that the purpose of education is to acquire skills, to service industry, to develop entrepreneurship and ultimately to prepare for employment. Educational systems and ideologies are a product of the cultures they exist within and are therefore contingent on the times and locations in which they are conceived; for example, self-expression is a particularly modernist ideal, whereas a focus on skills acquisition is a particularly neoliberalist agenda.

The principles we align with, whatever they may be, are ultimately a reflection of a personal philosophy of education, who it is for and what purposes it serves: the individual, society, communities, the state, the market or industry. What then is the role of the illustrator-educator and what relationship does the educator have with the learner? Master, seer, trainer, guide, guru, expert, facilitator, enabler or information provider are all possible characteristics of the teacher-learner relationship. Reflection on teaching and learning experiences personally encountered, particularly those recognised as productive and/or challenging, can help inform a personal pedagogic approach.

Illustrators wishing to work in an educational capacity should understand teaching to be a distinct and highly skilled discipline. To be recognised as professional educator requires specialist training, particularly when working with vulnerable groups or children. Many illustrators do work across both disciplines professionally as teacher-practitioners. However, illustrators wanting to incorporate educational elements into their practice without being professional educationalists need not necessarily hold formal qualifications. Having some awareness of pedagogic theory will help to navigate different schools of thought, strategies and methods, allowing informed decisions to be made.

What is an education space?

Consider the lecture theatre or the classroom which are, for many, familiar educational spaces. The educator is positioned at the front of the space, a singular figure who conveys their knowledge on a particular subject – this may be done orally and visually. The 'learners' are numerous, sat in rows, often in chairs that can't be repositioned. Their aim: to subsume knowledge for later use, possibly during an exam or assessment. This arrangement assumes certain hierarchical relationships between teacher and learner, and reflects a particular pedagogic ideology. The spatial learning environment, its location, design and organisation, dictates and augments the learning experience.

Education does not only happen within designated spaces such as classrooms or lecture halls; teaching and learning also occurs in the corridors, canteens, playgrounds and staff rooms of nurseries, schools, colleges and universities. Neither is learning confined within formal educational institutions; museums, libraries, galleries and places of embodied knowledge are also learning spaces. Indeed, any place where people congregate – the home, the internet, meeting halls, places of religious workshop, youth clubs, street corners, etc – can all be considered spaces for education. Educationalist and social historian Colin Ward advocated the urban environment as a location for learning, engaging children in issues and decision-making that affected the planning and construction of the cities they inhabited. Some have been more radical in their critique of the institutions and spaces in which we learn. Philosopher Ivan Illich called for a total reinvention of the spaces and methods of schooling, arguing that the design of these institutions was actually having the reverse of the intended effect.

Questioning what is a teaching and learning space will allow the illustrator to select the most appropriate location or space for their pedagogic activity. This decision may be an ideological or conceptual one, or one based on practicalities such as where the intended learners habitually congregate. This may involve working with an existing institution or community, or constructing an institution or situation specifically for this purpose.

Signature pedagogies

Even if the intention is not to teach illustration skills, illustrators wanting to facilitate learning activities and environments can reflect on the methods frequently used when teaching and learning illustration. There are several signature pedagogies particular to illustration that are transferable and adaptable.

STUDIO LEARNING AND COLLABORATION
Peer learning is widely recognised in pedagogic theory for its ability to foster communities of practice within which different types of knowledge are recognised and valued. Embedding learning strategies, such as group work, negotiation and shared responsibility, are attributed to mirroring the world of work. While these pedagogic strategies are universal, the relevance to illustration practice is particularly pronounced. From the outset, illustrators are informed that their work is based on a series of collaborative relationships. Illustrators are naturally suited to working within collaborative dynamics. Consider the studio culture within which

---

<u>Cooperative learning</u>
Students learn by working in groups towards a common goal. By learning cooperatively, students are able to learn from and use each other's skills and knowledge. The teacher facilitates learning rather than just imparting information. Cooperative learning was notably advocated by educator Paulo Freire (1921–1997) in *Pedagogy of the Oppressed* (1968) as a method to counteract the oppression he saw during his experience teaching literacy skills to adults in Brazil.

illustration is taught. Collaboration is emphasised with spaces often specifically curated to facilitate discursive environments. Students are frequently asked to negotiate and liaise with one another to produce joint projects with the intention of emphasising the diversity of ability within a collective team. Learning is a social activity.

DIALOGUES Much of the student illustrator's educational experience involves having to verbally articulate and deliberate ideas. Discursive learning activities, such as tutorials, presentations and peer-led discussions, are often imbedded into programmes of learning. During these exercises, student illustrators will showcase creative outcomes in progress while engaging in conversations with peers and tutors to demonstrate their learning and development. The ability to explain rationales, pitch ideas and defend decisions with candor is a valuable interpersonal skill. The ability to communicate with clarity, both verbally and through creative practice is particularly valuable when needing to engage diverse groups of people. When leading educational activities, illustrators can apply this skill to ensure instructional direction and project aims and intentions are understood. Illustrators can also facilitate comfortable and social working environments through fostering discussions around subjects and themes being explored. Creating 'low risk' working environments in which people feel free to share opinions without judgement, ask questions and admit difficulty will help groups feel at ease and thus more willing to engage with tasks, particularly if they are new to the task at hand.

MAKING-BASED RESEARCH

Student illustrators are taught to synthesise several research methods. When submitting portfolios for examination, they are often asked to demonstrate their learning process by including development work that has informed the realisation of their projects. This preparatory content, made while exploring the subject matter, is creative, experimental and diagnostic. It is not only proof of rigour but a demonstration of individual creative and cognitive development. The strategies used in the process of idea development can form the foundations of transferable exercises, which can help facilitate others to also acquire new skills or investigate a concept through creative investigation.

INSPIRATIONAL DISPLAY MAPPING Wall spaces in studio environments, particularly those situated near desks and work areas, are often used to display inspirational images and objects. The content may relate to one or a number of projects and/or have been collected due to a tacit attraction that may come into relevance at an indeterminable time. These inspirational constellations are individual to the practitioner charting conceptual and visual landscapes and/or serving as research inventories. Displays may consist of any manner of content such as found or collected print ephemera, the work of other artists, debris, found objects, material samples and so forth. Curating these displays is a visual demonstration of research interests. They are usually located within the working environment so they remain in direct sight and are easily viewed, be it for direct reference or as a enigmatic backdrop, helping to focus and guide the working process. Contemplating displays as a whole allows for chains of associations to be revealed and unforeseen connections to be made.

STUDIO WALLS
*Of jeweller Lina Peterson
and artist Jasleen Kaur*

EDUCATION

Signature pedagogies

STUDIO WALLS
Of illustrator Rachel Lillie

COLLABORATIVE ILLUSTRATIONS
Nick White and Ed Cheverton

In this ongoing project, Nick White and Ed Cheverton explore the potential of collaborative illustration practices. Each illustrator posting the other the start of a collage to respond to and finish, the result, a vast collection of collage works that blur their otherwise distinctive practices. The visual responses are varied; playful or witty textual retorts are offset with solely compositional replies. Mimicking the collaborations that can happen naturally in the illustrator's studio environment, White and Cheverton have entered into a dialogue long distance, creating a framework for visual discussion and play.

Community of practice

A concept developed by educationalist Étienne Wenger (b. 1952) to describe formal and informal social groups who share a common craft, profession or concern, and therefore can learn together by exchanging knowledge and experiences.

EDUCATION

Signature pedagogies

COLLABORATIVE ILLUSTRATIONS
Nick White and Ed Cheverton

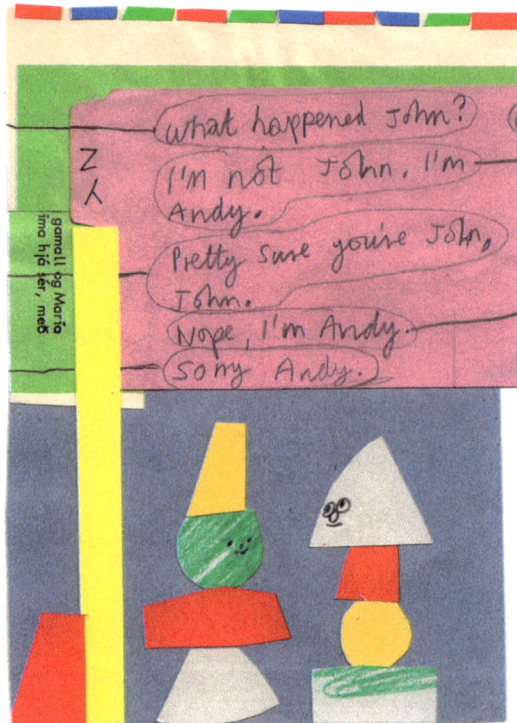

Shop talk

The workshop as an educational experience conceived and facilited by illustrators is addressed here as a distinctive method not to be confused with an activity the illustrators themselves undertake in order to acquire new skills. The illustration-led workshop may operate in a number of ways, for example:

— Illustration outcomes and artefacts are to engage participants in a workshop activity. This approach might use a specific illustrative practice, usually the facilitator's, to encourage discussions, creative activities, or to engage groups with topical issues, locales or institutions.

— A workshop activity is designed with the intention of gaining knowledge, insight or information from specific targeted participants. This information will then be interpreted and represented through the illustrator's creative practice. This method is akin to social research or ethnographic methods.

— Workshop participants co-author or collaborate on creative works with the facilitating illustrator. In such cases a degree of control will have to be relinquished to accommodate the desires of the participant, and a variability of quality should be anticipated. Be sure to gain consent and credit all collaborators appropriately in all public uses of jointly-produced work.

Illustrators might find themselves delivering workshops as part of an institutional educational, outreach or engagement programme. In such circumstances, hosting organisations may stipulate specific requirements relating to their individual agendas. Participants may also have particular expectations which may not align with those of the illustrator. Workshop organisers are increasingly opportunistic and entrepreneurial when finding locations and environments to host activities. Participatory activities can take place in any location where people are able to congregate undisturbed. These might be public or private venues, municipal spaces, rooms hired within cultural institutes, commercial properties etc.

When using locations that belong to or are under the control of outside agencies, such as schools, institutes, local councils etc, it is important to be mindful of the wider communities you are working among and the others using those spaces. Fostering relationships and gaining trust take time and effort but will ultimately lead to meaningful and fruitful collaborative experiences.

When developing workshop activities, deciding upon the intended outcomes often comes first; an artefact, creative response, new knowledge, learning experience, engagement opportunity etc. Despite this planning, the results of any workshop remain, to an extent, unpredictable, and you will often find yourself 'going with the flow' with outcomes that can deviate from what is expected. This does not mean the experience has not been valuable. Making mistakes or arriving at different solutions is often an influential learning experience.

MATERIAL OUTCOMES   Workshop outcomes can often be intangible and hard to document, for example when results entirely experiential and/or artefacts are a by-product of the process. Often, learning is not exemplified in the material outcomes but occurs during the experience of discussion, negotiating with others, making, trial and error. This can make 'results' and

---

Play

Educationalist and inventor of the kindergarten system, Friedrich Fröbel (1782–1852), developed a set of theories that promoted play within early years education. He recognised the importance of encouraging imaginative and creative engagement with materials and the world, particularly for young children.

Constructivist learning

The concept of knowledge as constructed, rather than passively acquired, through personal experiences. Meaning is constructed by making connections between new experiences and prior knowledge. Key theorists in this area are Jean Piaget (1896–1980) and Lev Vygotsky (1896–1934); the influential work of educational reformer John Dewey (1859–1952) is thought to form the foundations of constructivist thought.

'successes' difficult to measure, evaluate and sometimes even recognise, as the benefits of learning can only much later be realised and/or applied. The institution you are working with may require 'artefacts' to demonstrate impact – this might be required to fulfil funding requirements, to evidence to trustees, to maintain charity status, etc. Evidence of 'success' (i.e. through a material outcome) can also be beneficial to participants helping to make the process of learning tangible. Cultural Institutions are often committed to engaging diverse audiences in order to widen the social demographic of their patrons. When invited or hoping to work with groups who might have complex needs consider whether, as an illustrator, you have the appropriate training, experience and aptitude.

HERITAGE AS PROCESS: CONSTRUCTING THE HISTORICAL CHILD'S VOICE THROUGH ART PRACTICE, 2016
Rachel Emily Taylor
Artist residency and exhibition at The Foundling Museum

As part of her practice-based doctoral research, Rachel Emily Taylor devised and led creative workshops to explore how heritage and historical narratives of childhood experience could be animated in the contemporary moment.

Using narratives within the museum's collection for inspiration, child participants used performative role play techniques to invent a 'foundling' identity. The characters were then visualised through a pair of self-portraits painted by the children, depicting themselves both in the here and now and as their imagined foundling child. These workshop outcomes were then displayed alongside the museum's permanent displays, to provoke an understanding of the collections as accessed through the comprehension of children today.

Learning *through* illustration

Learning *through* illustration is distinct from learning *how to* illustrate. Learning through illustration uses illustration strategies and behaviours as tools to facilitate teaching and learning of other subjects such as science, geography, social history and maths.

This potential for learning *through* illustration has been acutely observed and utilised by educationalist Emily Jost, who has curated a unique programme of teaching and learning events and activities in her role as Head of Education at The House of Illustration, London. The potential of learning through illustration is most evident in the primary or 'early years' workshops Jost organises; integrated into school curriculum, illustration methods are used, for example, to teach the plant life cycle for Key Stage 2 (7-11 year olds). An illustrative brief is set, to create an illustration that accurately communicates to others the cyclical nature of plant development and reproduction. Workshops introduce students to low risk, accessible illustrative techniques. Some are technical (paper collage, mark-making) and others are distinctly more conceptual (visual analysis, interpretation and thinking). There are three identifiable stages of learning occurring within such experiences.

— Firstly, the intention to visually articulate what is understood requires deeper thinking. The act of drawing or image-making encourages a sophisticated sort of comprehension, one that involves a kind of internal visual *sense-making*.

— This is followed by a process of 'working out' and checking or confirming and understanding during the act of making. Gaps in knowledge and realisation of what is not understood is also revealed visually through this process.

— Finally, the illustrative outcome is used as a representation of a student's understanding and can be used to showcase this development to peers and adults. The illustrations also serve as prompts for dialogue around the subject matter through which erroneous knowledge can be corrected and wider contexts discussed.

RIDLEY ROAD MARKET
Emily Jost, Head of Education
House of Illustration

Children from Princess May Primary School, Hackney, document a local market, currently under threat of closure, by studying historic maps and photos and drawing in situ. Illustrator Sion Ap Tomos worked with the children for five days at the Hackney Archives and on location, and designed the resulting limited edition book, booklet and poster. The project was delivered as part of an Arts Council grant by House of Illustration.

Residency as method

Illustration residencies, while multifarious in form, conform to the following:

— The creative practitioner is situated 'on-site' for a prescribed period of time.

— Location and/or subject matter are often defined by the commissioning institution or governing body; the redevelopment of a specific site, an area of geological or natural significance, or a collection within a museum or gallery are familiar scenarios.

— Creative practitioners are selected by submission of a proposal or indication of intention and use it as an opportunity to engage with a new subject matter or exposure to new influences.

The purpose of a residency is often to foster links between a collection, institution, location and an audience, community or public body. This position is one of liaison or interpreter, a conduit through which information or knowledge is made accessible, available, understandable and/or engaging. Being resident allows for everyday observations, testing of concepts or prototyping on-site and being in direct contact with a community or landscape. Illustrators are particularly adept in these approaches, which are integral to much illustration practice, with communication, inclusivity and accessibility being core illustrative principles.

Residencies should not be seen as exclusive to cultural institutions; an office environment or workplace, for example, should be seen as equally relevant and applicable. These are the types of location that most interest illustrator, Christy Burdock. During her six-month residency at London's House of Illustration, Burdock observed and documented the working lives of its employees. Burdock paid particular interest to overheard conversations, preferring these to interviews, which she finds prohibits the openness of the interviewee, recording through notes and video. Language and associated behaviours, particularly of the 'inconsequential kind', are of most interest, as these are especially revealing of an individual's personal ideologies.

Burdock was drawn to Paula Rego's mural *Crivelli's Garden (The Visitation)*, which is the result of a residency of her own at the National Gallery and is said to depict staff working there. Like Rego, Burdock uses metaphor, allegory, myth and fables to depict interpersonal relationships and emotions, as well as the invisible power structures at play. Applying these 'masks' allows for her subject to see themselves reflected in the works, while preserving their anonymity. The Christmas party for House of Illustration employees was the inspiration for Burdock's largest work. Such ordinary, everyday situations are of greatest interest to Burdock as they allow her to shed the mantel of 'artist' and become an equal participant within the community she is researching. Burdock sees her role as one who illuminates dark corners of society, for both those she is working with and society at large.

HOUSE OF ILLUSTRATION RESIDENCY
Christy Burdock

EDUCATION

Residency as method

HOUSE OF ILLUSTRATION RESIDENCY
Christy Burdock

Documents of experience

Sharing experiences through autobiographical narratives takes many forms, and is used within different disciplines for reasons of rehabilitation, analysis or conflict resolution. For illustrators, this is not a therapeutic exercise but a method by which deeply personal or private events are documented for the singular purpose of informing others.

Such documents are used as tools to share knowledge and educate around complex or sensitive issues by sharing relatable experiences, challenging perceptions and/or evoking empathy. Stories of physical and mental health conditions, bereavement, gender, identity, and familial relationships are common subject areas. They may invite the audience to consider how they, or one of their loved ones, would respond if confronted with such a situation or simply shed light on lived situations outside of familiar experience.

Often diaristic in form, such narratives are conveyed from a first-person perspective with a focus on everyday experiences. Familiar forms are comic or graphic narratives, zines or publications, although this method does not prescribe a particular outcome, the only specification is that the outcomes can be disseminated freely, as accessibility is key. The use of diary-like prose, subjective opinion, humour and anecdotal storytelling can further aid engagement, particularly when describing traumatic or complex scenarios. Illustrated narratives of this nature are well positioned in the burgeoning graphic medicine literary genre, within the broader field of medical humanities, where it can provide medical professionals with insights into the emotional experience of patients. Comics in particular have been presented as a research method for clinical practitioners.

Matilda Tristram's graphic novel, *Probably Nothing*, exemplifies this method. A personal account of how, at eighteen-weeks pregnant, she was diagnosed with stage 3 bowel cancer. Tristram describes the process of her diagnosis and treatment and the day-to-day effects of her illness. Her illustrations, a combination of unassuming, naïve line and wash images and terse prose describe in almost mundane detail, unbearable day-to-day experiences with wry humour and acutely human observations. In doing so she challenges ideas about the perception of illness with the direct intention of others learning from her own experiences.

Illustrators understand the inherent power of visually telling stories and are aware of the agency this affords the illustrator. If the intention is to both educate and empower others, one possible strategy would be to design an infrastructure or environment that enables others to exercise the role of author, (auto)biographer or story teller. Illustration is used here to facilitate the voices of others and illustration methods are used as a way to formulate opinions and own world views, which can in turn be shared within own communities or more widely.

This method is exemplified by World Comics, created by Sharad Sharma, a 'grassroots' comics initiative that provides participants with the opportunities and skills to create their own graphic narratives as a vehicle to organise thoughts and make sense of their own lived experience. These are then disseminated within villages, meeting halls, schools and offices. Their aim is to strengthen democracy by providing a voice to marginalised peoples, silent minorities and those who are illiterate, in this instance from rural Indian communities. Utilising the inherent accessibility and economy of materials necessary for the comic strip format – a four-panel black-and-white A4 page cheaply reproduced on a photocopier – means

Reflective practice

Critical reflection and analysis of actions and experiences to continuously learn and improve in desired endeavours.

there are no barriers to participation. Stereotyping, corruption, health, corporal punishment and discrimination are discussed freely within the narratives. While the stories may tackle global issues, these comics are relevant to those who are reading them because they are local stories and therefore highly relatable.

WORLD COMICS
Sharad Sharma

MANDIROGATORY

— RAHUL CHAUDHARY

Dialogic teaching

Using talk as a learning tool, encouraging discussions between teachers and learners, as well as peers, about their experiences, (mis)understandings and feelings.

PROBABLY NOTHING
Matilda Tristram
Published by Viking

FEBRUARY

I was wearing my favourite T-shirt on the day of the diagnosis. I never want to wear it again.

The flat is full of flowers.

We all cram round our tiny kitchen table and start getting used to things. 'The great thing about your tiny kitchen is that I can reach anything without leaving my seat!'

Mum tells us something about her PhD; 'It was the publisher who censored it, not the translator at all!'

No one can bring themselves to write 'cancer' in a card.

Apart from one friend who's had it before.

Lots of people send lovely messages.

And not so lovely ones.

I get annoyed when people ask if they can pray for me. 'Do it if it makes you feel better!'

And when people I don't know very well ask me how I'm feeling. 'How do you fucking think I'm feeling!?'

And when people send me emails about miracle cures. 'Lemon peel? Broccoli? I've been eating broccoli my entire life!'

And when everyone wants to visit me all at once. 'I don't want to see ANYONE!'

I lie on the bed in a patch of sun and remember lying on a rock by the sea at Point d'Endoume in Marseille.

Me and Tom talk about the other holidays we'll go on and I cry.

Tom fixes a tyre and I mend my slipper on the front step. It's good to be outside.

Brian Cox on the iPad helps me to fall asleep at night.

My parents and Tom come to collect me the next morning. 'Darling, you look so much better!'

The surgeon arrives. 'Matilda, everyone, if you'd like to follow me...'

A tiny, windowless room. I try not to think: 'It must be bad news.'

'The bad news is that I'm afraid the tumour was cancerous.'

I don't feel anything.

'The good news is that of the 25 lymph nodes we removed, only 5 were infected.'

'So we'll give you a course of mild chemotherapy to mop up any leftover cells.'

I am surprised to notice that the only reaction to being told I've got a potentially terminal disease is that my neck feels suddenly icy cold.

I think, 'This is the moment we hug each other and cry.'

'I'll let you have some space for a bit.'

We hug each other and cry.

We're quickly moved to a private room off the ward and brought cups of sweet tea.

Mum's got some Ritter Sport.

I have a CT scan to see if it's spread to my liver or lungs.

It hasn't.

Illustration-based research

Practise-based research is capable of bringing scholarly inquiries to broad interdisciplinary and non-specialist audiences. Illustrative strategies can be used to bring together different bodies of knowledge in order to present and communicate multifaceted perspectives surrounding a particular subject matter or concern. As a creative form of representation, illustration can inhabit many contexts and environments – art venues, educational institutes, in the home as artefact or ephemera, etc. As multi-operational artefacts, such works can attract audiences to engage with a variety of intentions. They may be enjoyed for their merit as simulating artworks and/or be seen as a creative vehicle for analysis and debate. The materials, processes of production and creative representation used in their creation can also contribute meaning to the themes and concerns discussed. Realised through illustrative forms, works can be experienced in situ, for example within an exhibition or workshop activity, but can also be archived or held in collections for future posterity as valid representations of knowledge.

ELSEWHERE
Esther McManus
Produced as part of the Stray Voices Project and Being Human Festival, Institute of Historical Research, School of Advanced Study, University of London

Elsewhere documents a shared experience of walking the Great North Road between the two English towns of Stevenage and Hitchin. The journey retraces part of the same route made by the nineteenth-century journalist James Greenwood, documented in his booklet *On Tramp* (1883). During this period, the path was frequented by migrant labourers following the haymaking season toward the north of the country. Greenwood made the journey disguised as a fellow labourer to effectively observe the conditions and experiences of people then known as 'vagrants'.

Within *Elsewhere* a descriptive text brings Greenwood's writings into the present moment and into dialogue with current debates on homelessness, and in doing so captures the sense of a collective group walking, talking and contemplating together. In accordance with the text is a visual recording of the terrain, photographs and drawn illustrations, as well as details from maps and archival documentation held in collections at the The Senate House Library, UK.

McManus prepared for the project by sourcing historical materials relating to vagrancy laws and the use of common land, which could then be understood alongside contemporary documentation of the route. The content and physical production of the publication presented through McManus' illustrative rendering draws together contributions from various interdisciplinary specialists both academic and professional as well contributions from the general public. With Greenwood's account in mind, writing and discussion workshops held during the journey prompted questions surrounding language, 'othering' and the relationship between 'us' and 'them' and the impact of terms such as 'vagrant'.

The breadth of diversity present in the production of the project is also in keeping with a wider mandate to not only challenge how histories deemed marginal are recorded and described, and under what authority, but also diversifying the accessibility of this knowledge. *Elsewhere* emphasises how representations of academic knowledge can extend beyond, and even challenge, conventions that are so often purely textual, such as the peer-reviewed paper or essay, and are often only accessible to very limited peer groups. The publication conveys multiple perspectives by drawing together different types of knowledge: archival research, anecdotal stories and the shared experience of walking. The methods of production and the form of the printed leaflet also carry meaning by aligning the project with socio-political activities such as the history of print, independent publishing and creative activism.

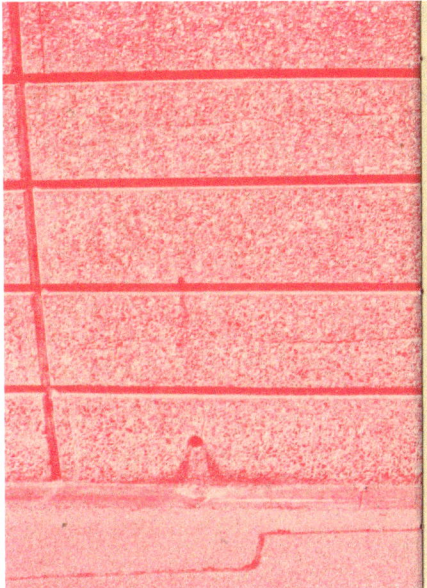

Experiential learning

A cyclical process involving reflecting on concrete experiences, learning from the experiences in order to identify the appropriate next course of action.

EDUCATION

Illustration-based research

ELSEWHERE
Esther McManus

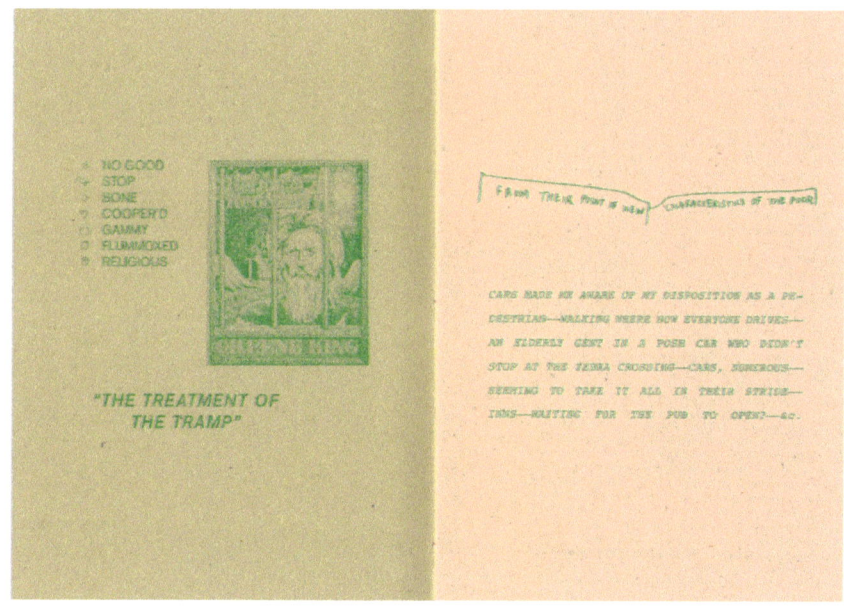

Data visualisation

Data visualisation or journalism is the process of using illustration to communicate trends and/or narratives that have been identified within a data sample. While an illustrator may not be directly engaged in the process of data collection, they may be called upon to interrogate existing information requiring interpretation and eventual visualisation.

Data graphics are often associated with diagrams, pie charts and graphs, however, these are by far not the only solutions. The illustrator's role may be to make an audience aware of a particular issue, to make new comparisons or to support a change of opinion or viewpoint. Increasing digitalisation of everyday living means that information of a range of subjects and aspects of human experience is now more readily available than ever. The accessibility of this data can leave it open to misinterpretation. Casting a critical eye and interrogating data samples with a few knowing questions can guide responsible interpretation, reveal patterns and trends, and in turn help identify the most appropriate means of visual representation. As a starting point the illustrator-researcher might consider:

— If the information is sourced from human participants – what is the sample size, demographic, location of these people?

— What forms of questioning have been used to obtain this information, i.e. structured interview, questionnaire, etc. and what impact might this have on the content of the response?

— Is the research funded, sponsored or aligned with any public or private organisation?

— Who commissioned the data; may there have been an agenda or vested interest?

Depending on the context of the project you may have more or less influence in what messages are communicated. The stipulations of the brief may be very prescriptive within a commissioned situation, and it will be necessary to consider the needs of both the clients and the audiences and make decisions accordingly. It is important to remember that data, whether it be in the form of numbers, percentages or statistics, all relates in some way to the human experience. Therefore, it may be more engaging and relevant to formulate a visualisation that is suggestive of a sense of humanity. These illustrative decisions may be informed from the insight gained during the research process. It might be the case that within the project there is opportunity to offer criticisms or alternative readings.

DEAR DATA
Giorgia Lupi and Stefanie Posavec

Each week for a year, Giorgia Lupi and Stefanie Poșavec collected and measured personal data – moments of indecision, laughter or goodbyes. This data was translated visually on the front of a postcard, on the reverse is a key that allowed the recipient to decode the information. Lupi and Posavec then mailed the postcards to each other's respective homes in New York and London, traversing the Atlantic in what they call a 'type of "slow data" transmission'. This data is personal, the use of the drawn line and handwriting emphasising the intimate nature of the information gathered.

DEAR DATA
Giorgia Lupi and Stefanie Posavec

Data visualisation

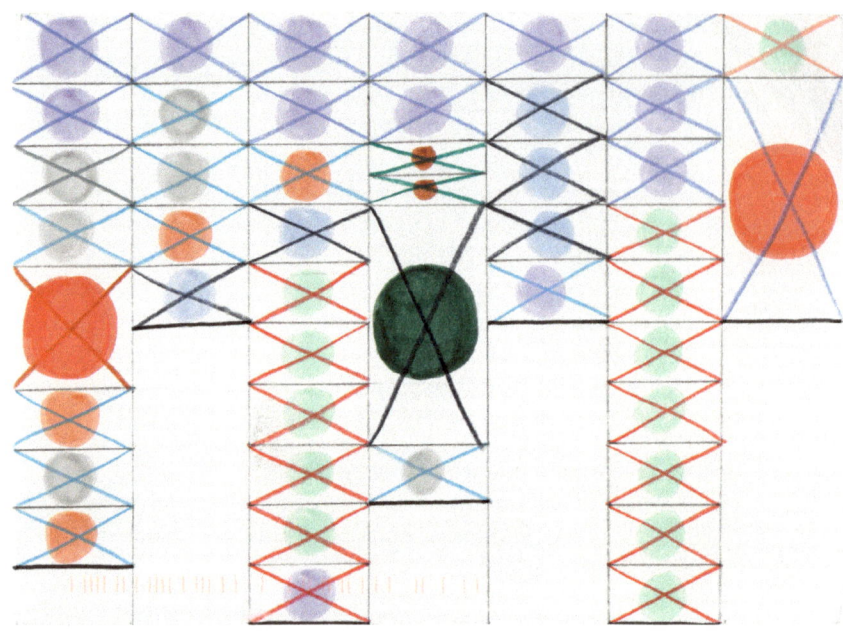

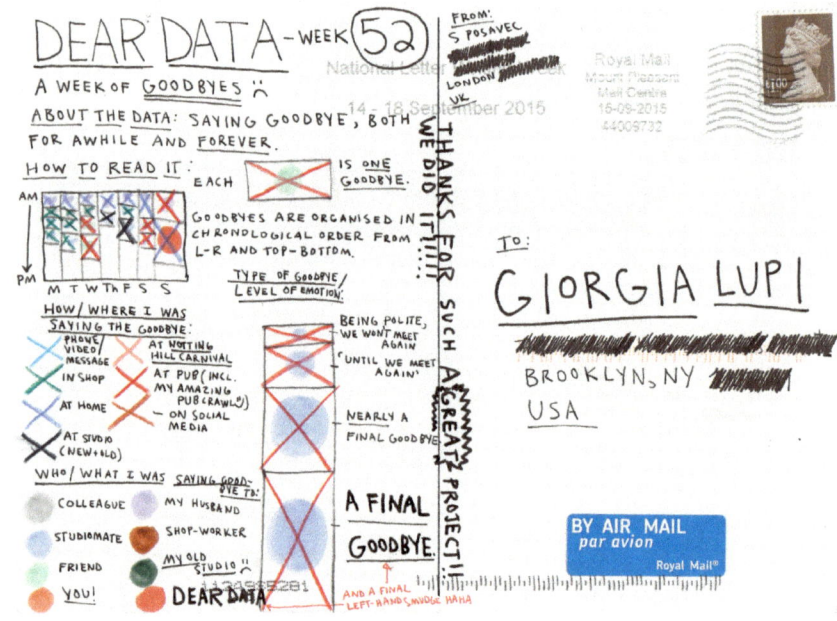

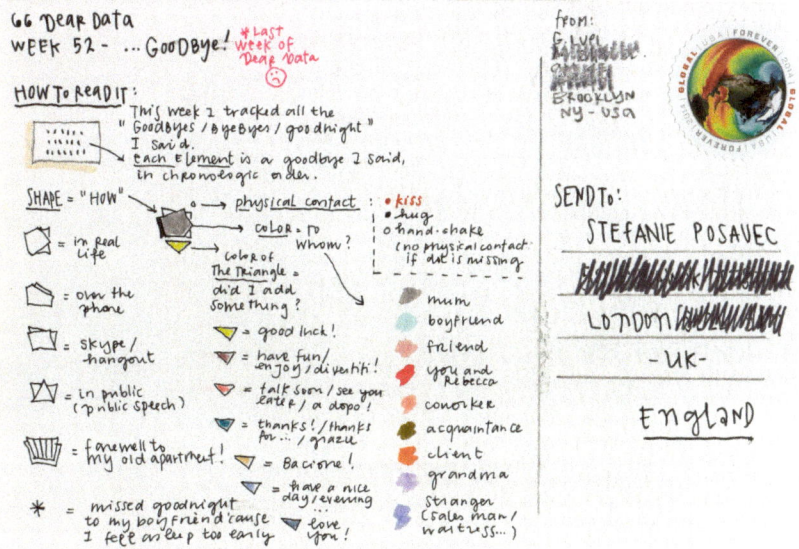

EDUCATION

Data visualisation

CONCRETE.RIP
Gareth Barnett, coded by Ben Neal
For the Common Ground Artist Residency at The New Art Gallery Walsall

Black viscous substance pours over a rotating 3d-scanned concrete fragment, from the now demolished Birmingham Central Library (UK). Opened to the public in 1974, Birmingham Central Library's concrete brutalism embodied a utopian vision for new towns centred around the automobile, and coincided with a dramatic shift in global oil prices and the beginning of a much more unstable market based on speculative future contracts, more than the simple laws of supply and demand.

Data is coded so that both the flow of oil that pours onto the fragment and the speed at which it spins responds to real-time fluctuations in the price of oil. This live animation visualises the complex and often invisible relationships between financial markets and the built environment.

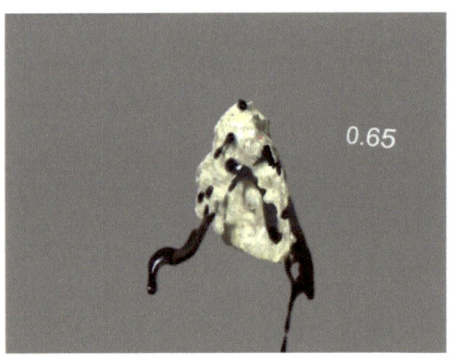
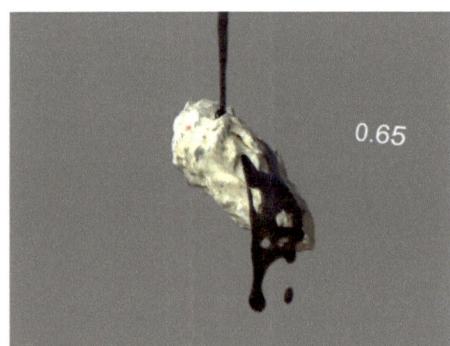

The language of reliability

Diagrammatical and instructional illustrations have a firmly-held association with reliability and authority. They are used to describe factual information or to aid comprehension of complex systems, procedures or processes and can be used independently of, or as a support to, written description.

Informative illustrations can act as a resource to be referred to in moments of urgent need, particularly when other help might be unavailable and the task at hand is an independent endeavour. To be effective, these illustrations must be clear and coherent, particularly if intended to be used in high-risk situations, for example, during emergencies when healthcare or safety procedures must be performed both efficiently and accurately. In such circumstances, instructional illustrations must be clear and coherent to audiences with potentially limited or no previous experience of the procedures they describe. Pictorial instructions are also used to support comprehension of techniques described by written texts alone. In the case of DIY manuals or cookery recipes, imagery can elucidate tricky processes; help identify and resolve problems and offer a comparative representation by which to determine success.

Representations of information through illustrative devices, such as flowcharts, pie charts and graphs, are often the only occasional illustration in any recognisable form, and are situated alongside non-literary texts or used by non-creative practitioners to articulate their knowledge with clarity and ease. Due to their practical applications, these methods of literal representation are instantly recognisable to lay audiences as visual languages of non-fiction, accuracy, authenticity and verifiable truths.

VISUALISING INVISIBLE OCEANIC LANDSCAPES
Sarah Langford

Illustrator and academic Sarah Langford, has been working in collaboration with the Natural Environment Research Council's National Oceanography Centre (NOCs), and the University of Southampton's Ocean and Earth Science department, to utilise illustration in the development of interdisciplinary teaching aids.

Working directly with Ocean and Earth Science Researcher Dr. Esther Sumner, Langford devised a series of workshops to support Sumner's students in understanding non-visual oceanic landscapes and geological phenomena. Acknowledging the limitations of diagrams, verbal or written explanations, and without the option of film and photography, Langford recognised the potential of illustration to aid comprehension of complex and invisible natural processes. The workshops introduce a series of oceanic geological phenomenon that participants are asked to interpret visually using illustrative strategies such as expressive mark-marking, narrative image-making and sequence. These have been piloted by academics and students from diverse backgrounds including the visual arts, illustration, Earth sciences and archaeology.

The project explores how engaging in the process of illustration to describe non-visual phenomenon and theory can support learning. The visual outcomes of the workshop can also then be developed into teaching aids for future use. Here, students, researchers and academics from different disciplines are brought together to exchange knowledge and expertise with mutual educational benefit.

6 EDUCATION

The language of reliability

VISUALISING INVISIBLE
OCEANIC LANDSCAPES
Sarah Langford

194

EDUCATION

**VISUALISING INVISIBLE
OCEANIC LANDSCAPES**
Sarah Langford

The language of reliability

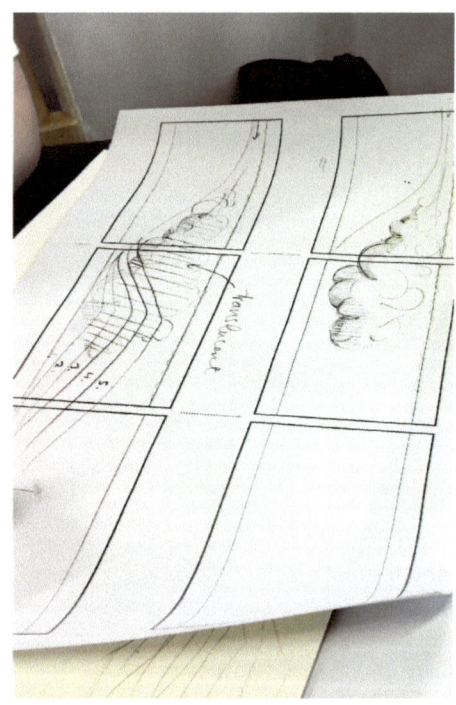

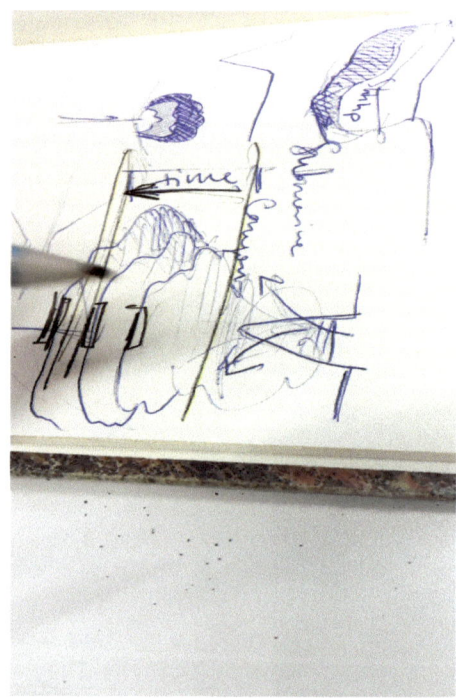

Interactive illustration

Illustrative outcomes used for educational purposes typically communicate using passive, didactic or instructional means – examples include narrative images, diagrams, schema or plans. Information is relayed through combinations of texts and images that are read or viewed and understood by the learner.

Pedagogic theory acknowledges that individual learners learn differently, that there is, in fact, a taxonomy of learning styles and no one tool, system or structure fits all. We may therefore consider that illustration, too, must be adaptable to different learning styles, to acknowledge that these more familiar methods of communication may not be effective, nor suitable, for all occasions and all learners. John Dewey, David Kolb and Paulo Freire, among many other educationalists, psychologists and philosophers have all advocated for the value of experience within education – a fundamental shift from the focus being on outputs and answers to situations and experiences. Social philosopher John Dewey, in particular, espouses learning through active experimentation, and the importance of understanding the role of individual experience within education.

Such a shift may seem like a move into unchartered territory for illustrators. To understand an experience, intangible and temporal, as illustration, is a decided move away from the illustration image or even from artefact. But consider the seminal work of illustrator Eric Carle, *The Very Hungry Caterpillar*, where a dye-cut hole in each page encourages the early reader to perform the character of the caterpillar with his or her finger, as he munches his way through apples, pears, chocolate cake and Swiss cheese; interactive illustrations published in 1969 teaching counting, food stuffs and metamorphosis.

Those who wish to utilise experiential learning methods within their illustration practice can consider a variety of possible communication tools: audio, visual, tactile, performative, kinetic and practical. Touch, movement and sound can be explored alongside the aesthetic and the visual.

PLAY_LEARN
Darryl Clifton
Camberwell College of Arts, UAL

An eight-foot-tall plush toy bear has a zip running down the centre of its body, providing access to removable internal organs made from felt. A bouncy castle with an entrance surrounded by teeth leads to a cavernous space representative of a stomach or small intestine, with rubber walls lined with gastric rugae and villi. A set of miniature wooden blocks are arranged like a small hamlet sitting upon a shifting platform, movable through a series of cogs and cams imitating the seismic shifts occurring during an earthquake. These are just three examples taken from the numerous outcomes for the *Play_Learn* project curated by Darryl Clifton, Programme Director of Illustration at Camberwell College of Arts, UAL. The brief: an interactive learning project, which asks BA Illustration students to produce an object, experience or thing that teaches an audience something concrete, asking the illustrator to consider using participatory or experiential means of communication specifically within the educational environment.

Students are given a theory, issue or system to communicate – the digestive system, string theory, earthquakes, the financial crisis of 2008 – deliberately slippery, confusing, contentious or highly complex. The project begins with exhaustive research, and with the illustrator becoming an expert in a particular field.

EDUCATION

Interactive illustration

Explorations into how to communicate this information refer to *illustration as interactive artefact*, in which both the 'user' (note, not reader) and the illustration have an effect on each other, and there is a two-way flow of communication. Such illustrative artefacts demand some form of physical engagement: touch, sound and smell.

With emphasis placed on how materials feel or react to touch, many of these projects focus on materials and their tactile properties – the comforting velour of a plush toy utilised to engage younger audiences, or the reassuring stability of a beautifully engineered wooden construction. The growing accessibility of nascent coding languages and Arduino means that simple digital interactive experiences are constructed with relative ease and can be used to create interactive experiences.

Simultaneously, the brief asks illustrators to consider how *they* learn and reflect upon the experiences they have had. Research into pedagogic theories surrounding experiential learning often leads students to play as a method to learn. Play is increasingly valued as a pedagogic method and has become a mainstay of early years education. Play is about following a set of pre-prescribed rules, conditions or instructions and operating creatively within these parameters; it is therefore a familiar learning experience for many illustrators. Play involves suspending reality, and the creation of imaginary scenarios or worlds, reinventing new relationships and new ways of working. Play involves risk, but is suggestive of risk with a safety net, and is not necessarily synonymous with flippancy or glibness; intentions may be rational, serious even.

Outcomes for the brief are multifarious in form: games, toys, environments, exhibits, books and performances. The form is selected for its appropriateness to the message being communicated as well as the intended audience and environment. From schools to museums to the home, each educational space offers differing concerns that are carefully considered. Schools, for example, have specific curriculums that they must adhere to, therefore successful application in this environment relies on the illustrator having the knowledge of how their outcome will be used within this set framework.

Students are encouraged to test their outcomes on potential user groups throughout the production stages, and to gather feedback on how they function and communicate in the 'real' world with testing and prototyping ensuring efficacy in final outcomes.

PLAY_LEARN: BEAR AND ME
Lizzie Scarlett Towndrow

At the heart of Lizzie Scarlett Towndrow's practice is an interest in how knowledge can be passed on using our hands. This larger-than-life interactive bear was made using techniques Towndrow learnt during a series of internships with textile artists: knitting, quilting, patchwork, felting, carding – craft knowledge passed on through the act of doing. Towndrow organised a number of workshops with young children, which used the bear to learn about the body through making and doing; a work booklet that transformed into a 3d wearable costume accompanied the activity.

Bear and Me was produced as part of the Play_Learn project run by Darryl Clifton for BA Illustration students at Camberwell College of Arts, UAL.

PLAY_LEARN: PLAY-O-LOGY GIANT DIGESTIVE SYSTEM
Katie Rose Johnston and Charlene Man

The inflatable play space, *Giant Digestive System*, is the creation of illustrators and Play-o-logy founders, Katie Rose Johnston and Charlene Man. Interested in creating explanations for scientific ideas that are fun and experimental, Johnston and Man set out to challenge current educational methods by creating an interactive environment in which the audience needs to play and discover for themselves. Entering the pink, cavernous space of the *Giant Digestive System*, workshop participants experience the journey of digestion for themselves. Six tactile material panels depicting the stages of human digestion surround an inflated structure, suggestive of existing play environments, while also allowing for quick construction. Research into pedagogic theory was conducted alongside a detailed analysis of endoscopy, microscopic imagery and material experimentation, in order to create a work that is both engaging and informative.

Giant Digestive System was produced as part of the Play_Learn project run by Darryl Clifton for BA Illustration students at Camberwell College of Arts, UAL.

Interactive illustration

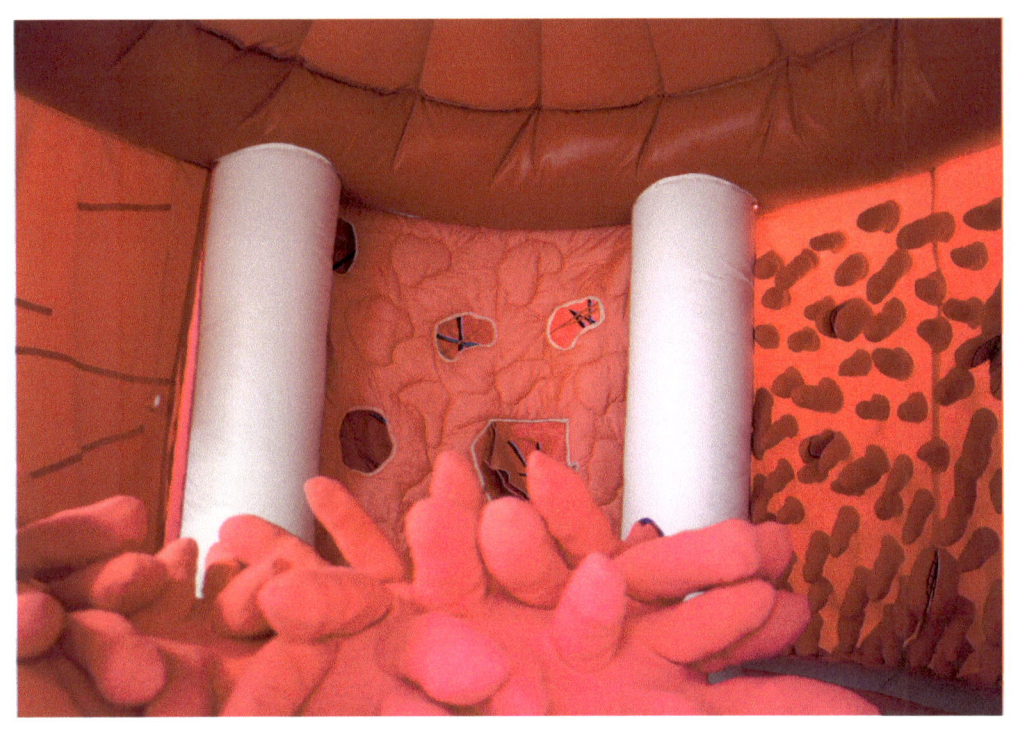

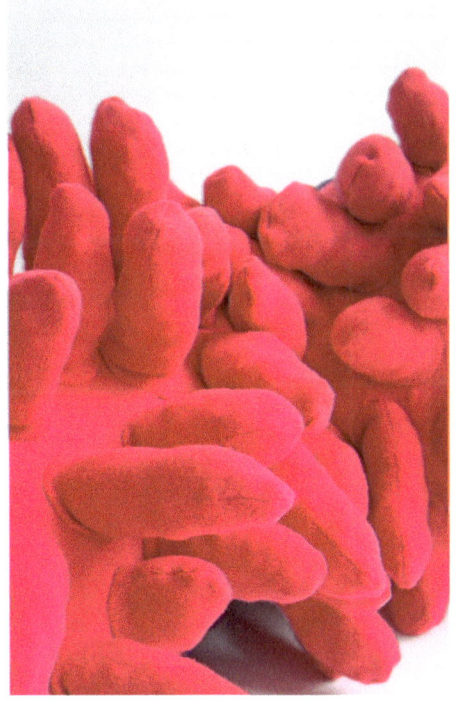

7 ILLUSTRATION FUTURES

ILLUSTRATION RESEARCH

IS

ENTIRELY COLLABORATIVE
AND CROSS-DISCIPLINARY,
AND IT EMPHASISES THE AGENCY
OF ILLUSTRATORS
AMONGST THEIR SPECIALIST COHORT.

ILLUSTRATION FUTURES

When the words you are reading (or listening to) now were yet to be written, and all that existed of this book was a collection of fragmented notes stored somewhere in the ether between two interconnected MacBooks, we, the authors of this text, searched far and wide in search of others who shared our vision and enthusiasm, secure in the knowledge that education is the answer. Travelling across both our national home turf and abroad, we visited as many illustration programmes as could grant us time. We did our best to arrive without judgement, although we are, after all, human. We were humbled by the warmth with which we were received, being understood was never a concern even when spoken languages failed across borders. Here, we had the benefit of our discipline on our side; the illustrator, if nothing else, is the communicator par excellence. We were invited to observe as guests, be among young scholars; there were chats, meetings, discussions too numerous to mention, and much of the time the best we could do was simply to listen. Our stance in writing this book has always been to temper the balance between aspiration and possibility. For all the impassioned proclamations, nothing can be achieved in the absence of an infrastructure for illustrators to exist within. However, theory, concepts, ideas are vital to change. Theory is not the anthesis of practice – it is the precursor of the action. Developing illustration theory will enable us to collectively develop the discipline into a new aesthetic form.

During our research we were fortunate enough to be hosted for three days by the independent educational programme Illustration Futures. The course, which refuses to ever be formally accredited, has been developed by a multi-specialist group of illustration practitioners, and now mentors thirty-six illustration scholars per academic annum. Organised at the turn of the last century, the collective began modestly as a series of informal social work evenings. Hosted after working hours in one another's studio spaces, the members would discuss and share projects in progress and critical writings. As the group grew in patronage, the sessions, too, diversified to include practical workshops, seminar series and a professional advice bureau, and the group took on the formal identity of Illustration Futures. Realising the potential of the momentum they had created, the education programme initially began with three, six-month scholarships, and Illustration Futures are proud to now support a full scheme of work across three academic years (which they describe as 'phases') that, on completion, is tantamount to an undergraduate degree course.

The philosophical mandate of the programme takes speculation as its starting point: what the future might hold for illustration, the various challenges and the potentials of infiltrating new contexts. During each phase, scholars choose sessions offered from within a series of modules including Interpretations, Connected Things and Containers in phase one. In phase two: Immaterial Practices, Conceptual Reckoning and Innovatory Methods. The final phase, Situated Practice, is entirely self-directed, during which scholars identify and implement their ideal professional futures. Sessions can run between a day and five weeks and address topical concerns such as *fictional histories, reading for illustration, engineering lifeworlds* and *is this real*? The supervision team stresses that ideas and making, as well as process and outcome, are indistinguishable. Illustration 'practice' is ubiquitous and realised across all methods of production: theoretical, creative making, writing and performance. A display of works in progress showcased a diverse array of future imaginings, including stories rendered through bespoke algorithms, VR sculptures, oil painting, performative print-making and sky projections. Scholars explained that no process is venerated over any other, 'because we are confident in our examinings of illustration, no materials, methods, processes or applications should be out of bounds, what matters rather is their relation and relevance to the ideas expressed'. Social relations within the programme are modelled on reciprocity rather than commodification or hierarchy. Scholars are asked to declare skills on arrival so they can donate and trade knowledge. Progression across the phases is understood as a broadening of expertise rather than a narrowing or specialisation. Time is scheduled each week for discussions without a preassigned agenda. Personal philosophies are developed though 'free talk', with topics frequently addressed concerning current affairs, including subjects such as global politics, economics, scientific development, the future of work and identity politics.

Transitioning scholars in the final phase often take on illustration residencies within institutions, organizations and businesses, where, by all accounts, they hold valued positions as interpreters, translators, imaginaries and social researchers. This pioneering scheme, the likes of which we had never encountered before, yields much success, often leading to further opportunities. The work generated by illustrators during the residencies has been used to inform company policy, elucidate complex systems, engage hard-to-reach audiences and support internal communications. Residencies have also led to companies employing in-house illustrators as permanent members of staff. We were surprised to find that the Illustration Futures programme made no mention of entrepreneurship, industry or business at any point in its course content or delivery. When we posed this query to the team they explained these terms are not relevant, as distinctions between life, university and 'work' are a fallacy. They were, however, keen to impress that they didn't imply that personal lives should be unbalanced by work, but instead that illustration should be understood as a tool valuable in all aspects of life and culture.

Illustration research is entirely collaborative and cross-disciplinary, and it emphasises the agency of illustrators among their specialist cohort. One illustration researcher we spoke to was currently working among a team consisting of architects, NGOs, lawyers and anthropologists to investigate, understand and visualise a reimagined prison system to encourage high rates of social rehabilitation. We also found illustration students engaged with projects that placed them among nurses in order to document patient experiences; with archivists to preserve personal histories of marginalised groups, and with city planners and engineers on a project that empowers children to redesign their own urban communities. An impassioned mission statement from the course curators reads: 'Questioning of the potentials of illustration has never been more urgent as we work to prepare students to enter into a rapidly expanding field … What are most needed are transferable and adaptable skills that facilitate intelligent work that has a place and can be applied in real, tangible, albeit diverse, contexts … Illustration is a collaborative discipline. It does not operate independently; it is made with the intent to engage. Illustration is a result of participation. Illustration Futures may have not yet arrived, but it is becoming.'

This gives us hope.

APPENDIX

PART 1: ADVICE AND HOW TO

208 — Proposals
209 — Working with others
210 — Interviews
212 — Reflective practice

PART 2: RESPONSIBLE PRACTICE AND ETHICS

213 — Positioning
   — Who benefits?
   — Legacy
214 — Informed consent

PART 3: KEY IDEAS

216 — Illustration research
   — Authorship
217 — Reporting
   — Crafting
218 — Activism
219 — Education

220 — Index
224 — Acknowledgements

IT IS THE RESEARCHER'S
RESPONSIBILITY TO ENSURE
THAT THEY CONDUCT THEIR STUDIES
IN A RESPONSIBLE MANNER,
TREATING OTHERS WITH
INTEGRITY,
RESPECT
AND
EMPATHY.

PART 1: ADVICE AND HOW TO

Proposals

Proposals are written with various and differing intentions – to convince, entice or inspire potential collaborators, funders, curators or employers. Proposals help clarify and formulate the intentions of a project and also help others understand and envision the work. Proposals may be necessary as part of grant applications, to access funding, to describe an academic project or to pitch ideas to a potential client. When writing a proposal, intentions should be clearly articulated, and written in straightforward and coherent language as appropriate to the proposal format.

Proposals are good opportunities to plan prospective projects. They require targets and logistical specifications such as time management and budgeting. It is important to consider all aspects of the project: materials, equipment, specialist help, etc. A proposal can place the illustrator in the role of project manager as well as creative producer in charge of finances and the wider project facilitation. Understanding the context, marketplace or audience for a project is an important part of any proposal process, and involves considering where the work is situated and why; how it will engage audiences and what the resulting impact will be.

PROPOSAL FORM

Project title (Working)

You and your work
— Context, how the project fits within your wider practice, are there common themes/concerns, etc?
— How does this project fit in with your work/practice/career trajectory?
— What relevant skills/experience/expertise do you have already?
— How will this project further existing skills?
— How does this project fit within the wider field of inquiry; is it comparable with similar projects by other practitioners or examples of good practice?

Methodology
— What are you going to do and how are you going to do it?
— How will research be conducted and why are these methods relevant?
— How will outcomes/ideas be explored or evaluated?
— Who are the people you will be working with, i.e. collaborators and/or participants?
— If working with others, is specialist training, clearance or permission needed to work with these people?
— What other expertise or training is needed to complete the project?
— Will interviews be conducted, if so do you need to get consent?
— What are the ethical considerations?

<u>Market, audience and public engagement</u>	— Where will the work be situated? Is there a particular location, environment or setting? — Is there a clearly identified market? — How will the work be publicised or promoted? — Is the work particular to a specific area within the industry: publishing, gallery, public engagement, etc.? — Who is the intended audience and why have you identified this group? — How will audiences be engaged? — What impact will the work have on the subject matter/audience/environment (as appropriate)?
<u>Timeline and project delivery</u>	— Chart a detailed timeline/calendar of work. This may change as you negotiate the demands of the project but should represent a realistic and achievable ambition. Be sure to factor in time for mistakes, experimentation and problem-solving.
<u>Finance</u> (<u>As applicable</u>)	— How much money (budget) do you need to complete the project? When costing a budget, consider material expenses, paying for services (including the help of any individuals working on the project), shipping and transport costs, as well as your own time. — Has any money been raised already? Funders can be more receptive when some of the money has already been granted or secured.
<u>Bibliography</u>	— A list of research references. This might include: gallery visits, books, existing case studies or projects. You can refer to sources that will be explored as well as those already investigated.

These points are not all encompassing and should be used as relevant to the project and application.

Working with others

Good communication is vital to the success of any group working together, and will ultimately benefit the project as a whole. There are many ways to work collectively. Consider the most efficient and appropriate ways to maintain clear channels of communication so that all involved have the necessary information and instruction required. Reflect on the most suitable ways to achieve this; it may require file sharing systems, regular briefing meetings, email updates, etc. It is likely that not all involved will be able to meet physically at one given time and place. Correspondence might have to be conducted online, in writing or through arranged phone conversations. When working within an international team be sure to consider time zone differences.

ORGANISING AND CHAIRING MEETINGS   The chair of a meeting helps guide and steer conversations to ensure all points are suitably met, and to manage group dynamics so that everyone has the opportunity to speak. Record meetings through keeping written notes or minutes; it may be helpful to have an external person doing this, if possible. If taking an audio recording, make sure all involved are aware and have given consent. When organising and/or chairing meetings consider the following:

Planning
— What is the intention of the meeting?
— Is a physical meeting really necessary, or would another mode of communication be more efficient?
— Write a detailed agenda outlining subjects to be discussed; prioritise topics for discussion by their urgency at that specific point in the project. This will help focus time so there is apt opportunity to discuss all areas necessary.

Setting up
— Ensure everyone is clear as to why a meeting is being held. Distributing the agenda prior to the meeting will help those attending to prepare in advance.
— Host meetings in locations that are conducive to what you want to achieve. Is the space accessible to all? Consider whether it is neutral, informal, formal, public or private. Does it reinforce authority hierarchies that will affect the outcomes of the meeting?
— The design of the space in which the meeting is held can enforce particular dynamics among a group: chairs in a circle, sitting round a table, facing an individual speaker, etc. Consider moving furniture and chairs, as possible, to ensure all feel comfortable and equal.

Afterwards
— When acting as chair, allow everyone apt time to express themselves, and be mindful that all have had the opportunity to speak.
— End meetings with positive resolutions.
— Records can be distributed post-meeting for reference, with any resolutions or points for further action highlighted.
— Identify a date for a next meeting if necessary.

Interviews

Before interviews can be conducted as part of a research process, some preparation will be required. While interviewing as a method is further discussed in Chapter 3: Reporting, the points raised here are reminders to support responsible practice and also to help gain the information appropriate to the research questions at hand. When interviewing people, it is important to know that the information gained may not be as expected, and it may not resolve projects. When organising an interview, consider the following:

Initial considerations
— What is the information you require?
— Who is best placed to provide you with this information?
— Are they willing to be interviewed?
— Will a sense of trust need to be established first? This can take time, the rationale for the inquiry should be transparent.
— Why is an interview the best method to gain the information

	you require? Is the information required available in any other way?
— Is the subject matter sensitive or upsetting? Is the interviewee made vulnerable by taking part? If so, can you ensure their well-being, safety and/or security?
Interview structure	— Who is being interviewed: a group, individuals, etc?
— What is the best way to converse with this interviewee(s)?
— Are they familiar with the interview process, i.e. an academic may be more used to discussing their area of expertise than a housewife discussing their daily life experience.
— Format your questions to help gain the most useful information.
— Closed questions that invite 'yes' or 'no' answers can be leading – this may or may not be desired.
— Open questioning that requires more elaborate explanation can lead to digressions but can also yield unexpected information.
— Using discussion points rather than questions can prompt more conversational content. This might lead to a more natural dialogue, but will also require steering to ensure content remains relevant.
Interview environment	— How does the location used impact on the interview dynamic?
— Does the interviewee feel secure and able to speak freely?
— Is the environment conducive to a productive meeting?
Group interviews	— Group interviews are an opportunity to capture dynamics that might help elaborate, or offer a range of perspectives, on a particular subject. Invite interviewees who share knowledge of a particular field or have knowledge that might be related to the views you are hoping to understand or bring together.
— Consider what is gained from bringing together a range of people. Are the opinions of a particular demographic required? Do they have similar or opposing knowledge or experiences? For example, interviewees can be grouped because they share a particular bond. They might be unknown to one another but have comparable knowledge of a particular subject. Interviewees might be asked to join a panel because they have different kinds of expertise that relate in some way.
— How will all participants be engaged? Some will be more confident speakers than others; consider whether the intention is to hear from all participants or to also examine the social dynamics operating within the group, in which case identifying quieter or more dominant voices might be a useful insight.
Recording	— How can the conversation be documented, for example: audio / visual, written notes, creative interpretation such as drawing?
— Why is this relevant or the most efficient method?
— For example, a voice recording will capture the words as spoken by the interviewee, written notes and visual re-

sponse can emphasise what the interviewer hears and interprets in the moment of hearing.
— Non-verbal communication can also be revealing of information, for example, body language, pauses and emotional response.
— How will interview recordings be stored? Are they secure and private? Will they be made public? Will they be destroyed after the project?

Reflective practice

Maintaining a reflective practice is valuable to all types of practice-based research where learning occurs through critical reflection during the act of making and doing. Donald Schön explains this process in *The Reflective Practitioner: How professionals Think in Action*, drawing upon the ideas of earlier educationalists such as John Dewey and David Kolb.

Kolb's dynamic reflective cycle describes the process of reflection in action in four stages: doing, reflecting, evaluating and testing. It is often compared to having a conversation with yourself, where sense is made of an individual's practice. The thinking and making process is tacitly implied within final outcomes, but without documentation, it disappears. Critical reflection ensures that processes are recorded and therefore can be drawn upon for future use. A synthesis of theory and practice is possible through reflective practice; the practitioner can articulate connections between the two through reflection, and one can be drawn upon to inform the other.

Practically, this process might involve keeping a reflective diary or journal; formats are varied and individual to the researcher; a notebook, journal, blog or video diary are all valid examples. Entries should be regular, although how often is again down to individual choice and practices. Possible contents of a reflective journal may include: contextual research, material experiments, descriptions of working processes, evaluation of experiences, accounts of progress, personal reflections, etc. Any contextual research, images of the work practitioners, articles, references, etc. should be accompanied by analysis and a description of why it is significant to the researcher's work. Use methods of reflection that are pertinent to the researcher's individual working process; reflective journals are personal and often not seen by anyone else, indeed it is often of little use to those outside of the project as it is specific and particular to the research being undertaken.

KEEPING A REFLECTIVE JOURNAL

Reflective practice involves using these four areas of questioning in order to document, analyse and aid progression:

1. What is the experience you have had: an interview, an experimental use of materials, a book you have read and analysed?
2. Reflect upon what you did. Why did you do it in that way? What were the results? What was positive or negative about the experience?
3. What can you conclude or learn from this experience? How well did it go? What was the reception from your peers or tutors?
4. Make a plan for how to progress. What will you do now? What will you try out next? What will you do differently?

PART 2: RESPONSIBLE PRACTICE AND ETHICS

All research has certain ethical implications to be considered. This process is integral within any research project. It is the researcher's responsibility to ensure that they conduct their studies in a responsible manner, treating others with integrity, respect and empathy. An indicator of good ethical practice is to question whether you are treating others, be they participants, audiences, colleagues or collaborators, in a way you would be happy to be treated.

Positioning

When acting as a researcher, positioning refers to the relationship and dynamic between yourself, your project and the subject(s) of your investigation. Power relations can be shaped through public discourses, media and institutions as well as human, social and cultural factors such as gender, race, religion, sexuality and different abilities. The illustrator researcher may approach their subject from a range of positions. These might be informed by subjective interpretation such as personal interests, their own areas of creative expertise, or their own personal experiences. The position the researcher adopts can inflect on the viewpoint, narrative and/or opinion described in the research project.

Ethnocentricity can be mitigated against by being self-aware of the factors informing your own knowledge, experiences and viewpoints. This reflection will allow you to recognise and confront your own prejudices and assumptions. A good practice is to simply be mindful that everyone is prejudiced and to consider how these might be informing the wider research project.

Who benefits?

A responsible practitioner considers who benefits from a research project and any outcomes. For example, how does a documentary project impact on the community being described; do they gain experiences, recognition or some other value from the project? Funding bodies, institutions and stakeholders might also benefit through their support or association with a project. What are the benefits to the illustrator conducting the project? Consider what will be achieved through conducting the project. Motivation is likely lead by a number of factors: to raise awareness of a cared-for cause; to obtain a higher academic achievement, to further employment opportunities. One rationale is not necessarily more worthy than another, but it is important to acknowledge the full spectrum of motives and potential impacts behind any work.

Legacy

Illustrators should be aware of the responsibilities they carry when making work about real people and lived experiences, be they living in the contemporary moment or distant past. Even the stories of the dead may have an impact in the here and now; relations may be living or affected by events long-past. How we document knowledge of ourselves and others carries the potential to leave a legacy. The information, messages and narratives, even the most seemingly mundane content conveyed in illustrative works, can be used to provide insight of the here and now to future societies.

Informed consent

First, ascertain who the participants within your project are. A participant may be the subject of research: those being documented or interviewed; a test audience for an illustrative work, etc. Participants should normally be given a choice as to whether or not they take part in your research, and informed consent should be sought, usually in written form. Institutions (whether academic or otherwise) may be able to provide ethics forms and pro forma consent letters, which can be adapted for specific use. Being on familiar terms with participants (a family member or friendship group for example) doesn't preclude them from ethical considerations, and informed consent should still be sought.

Gaining informed consent ensures that individuals have a clear understanding that they are participants in a project. Clear and plain language should be used in all records and correspondence to ensure clarity. Participants should be provided with copies of consent forms. Consent forms vary according to the nature of the research activity, but should specify:

— The name of the illustrator/researcher and brief project details including any working title.
— An invitation to participate and a brief description of the research activity, i.e. an interview, a workshop, a drawing exercise, etc.
— Permission to name participants (if necessary).
— Details of how the research activity will be recorded or documented.
— Details of how the information gained might be used, for example, will drawings be exhibited publically or published?
— Details of how this documentation will be stored and for how long.
— Contact details, should participants need to correspond after the research activity has taken place.
— The explicit right to withdraw their consent to take part after the research activity has taken place.

If working with at-risk groups such as children, vulnerable adults, etc, it may be necessary to gain additional consent from a parent or guardian. Working with an institute or organisation may require an application for ethical approval through their internal ethical committee. There are circumstances in which ethical clearance cannot be obtained, particularly when working covertly or in busy public environments. Consent may not be needed if there is no way an individual can be identified in the research outcomes.

INFORMED CONSENT FORM

Project title _____   Date _____

PARTICIPANT STATEMENT

	Yes	No
I confirm that I have read and understood the information sheet for this study dated [DD/MM/YYYY]. I have been able to ask questions, which have been answered satisfactorily and I have been informed of the purpose, risks and benefits of taking part in [Insert title of project].	○	○
I understand that my participation is voluntary, that I can refuse to answer any questions and that I can withdraw at any time without prejudice.	○	○
I understand that all information collected will be confidential and that any information that may be able to identify me (name, address, etc) will not be shared beyond the research team.	○	○
Contact information has been provided for the purposes of (1) obtaining further information from the researcher at any time, (2) to make a complaint and/or (3) to withdraw from the project.	○	○
I agree to being interviewed	○	○
I agree to the interview/activity being recorded in written notes	○	○
I agree to the interview/activity being audio recorded	○	○
I agree to the interview/activity being video recorded	○	○
I agree to being drawn	○	○
I agree to recognisable drawn images of myself being made public through exhibition and/or publication	○	○
I agree to anonymised transcripts of the interview being made public through exhibition and/or publication	○	○
I agree to anonymised audio of the interview being made public through exhibition and/or publication	○	○
I agree to my real name being used with quotes	○	○

Participant signature _____   Date _____

RESEARCHER STATEMENT

I have provided the participant with the information sheet for this study dated [DD/MM/YYYY]. I have explained this project to the participant, and the participant understands the implications of their involvement with the project. I understand that the participant has given consent freely.

Researcher signature _____   Date _____

PART 3: KEY IDEAS

Illustration research

015 Method
A tool, process or technique utilised to realise a specific aim.

015 Methodology
A strategic system or series of methods selected to conduct a sustained inquiry or to perform a task.

017 Analytical thinking
Methodical and logical thinking or reasoning; the ability to identify and solve problems.

019 Subjectivity
The principle of being open to multiple and variable interpretations.

021 Objectivity
Emphatic and verifiable interpretations of knowledge or information.

023 Qualitative research
Research processes using methods, often observation, which yield subjective feedback or data. The information collected is often descriptive and not numerical.

Authorship

027 Metaphor
A literary device in which one thing is used to poetically describe something else with which it is not immediately associated.

027 Narratology
A branch of criticism rooted in structuralist thought and linguistics, narratology is the systematic study and analysis of narratives and narrative structures and how we create, understand and are shaped by them. Narratology began with the writings of Vladimir Propp (1895-1970) and Mikhail Bakhtin (1895-1975); other key literary theorists who shaped our understanding of narrative theory include Roland Barthes (1915-1980), Algirdas Greimas (1917-1992) and Gérard Genette (1930-2018).

029 Autoethnography
A method of inquiry, analysis and representation in which the researcher reflects on their subject matter from their personal, first-hand experience.

029 Paratext
A literary term describing information surrounding and framing a main text or manuscript with the potential to influence the reader's interpretation, e.g. indexing, footnotes, appendices, etc.

031 Allegory

A storytelling device through which meaning extends beyond, or is disguised within, the presented narrative situation.

039 Lifeworld

The portrayal of a contained environment as defined by the subjective experiences of people, entities, situations and dynamics present within.

043 Linguistic turn

Recognition of the influence of language in constructing and informing meaning.

045 Author

A title attributed to an individual or group responsible for the production of a literary or creative work.

053 Semiotics
Rooted in linguistics, semiotics is a method for modelling the relationship between words and images, and for understanding how meaning is constructed. It can be used as a toolkit for understanding how visual communication works and the interpretation of signs. Charles Sanders Peirce (1839-1914) and Ferdinand de Saussure (1857-1913) founded the study of semiotics.

059 Death of the Author

An essay by literary theorist Roland Barthes (1915-1980) arguing that to assign an author to a text affects and limits the interpretation of the content.

Reporting

063 Anthropology

A discipline addressing all aspects of human life and culture with concerns as diverse and wide-ranging as religion, belief, gender relations, material culture, world views, domestic and family structures.

069 Ethnography

People-focused research, often utilising qualitative methods such as participant observation, interviews, focus groups and creative documentary methods in order to understand the lived experiences of others.

081 Anthropocene

A proposed epoch referring to the current geologic age in which human action has been dominant in influencing the development of the Earth's natural environment.

087 Flâneur (masculine) and Flâneuse (feminine)

A person who navigates and contemplates the urban environment through the act of leisurely wandering.

087 Psychogeography

An interdisciplinary field of inquiry most overtly bringing together psychology and geography, used to experience and navigate the city, urban and natural environments. Associated with the Situationist International organisation.

091 Dérive

A psychogeographical method in which a journey through an urban terrain is made on foot, guided only by emotional psychological impulses and encounters.

097 Ethnocentrism

The act of making pejorative or negative judgements of a perceived culture based on the observer's own preconceptions, values and world view.

099 Othering

The creation of a psychological divide between the concept of 'us' and 'them' through recognition of an observed or imagined difference between individuals or social groups.

101 Decolonising movement

Discussion, debate and activism aiming to highlight, address and debunk the insidious effects of colonialism within the systems and hierarchies influencing our societal and cultural institutions.

Crafting

105 The Bauhaus
Art school where founder Walter Gropius (1883-1969) and his peers reimagined art and design education with the intention to break down barriers and hierarchies between art and craft, and to engage with industrial production techniques.

107 Tangibility

Having actual material substance rather than being imaginary or speculative.

111 Aura

Coined by philosopher Walter Benjamin (1892-1940) as a quality relating to a presence in time and space, intrinsic within original artworks and impossible to capture through means of mechanical reproduction.

115 Medium is the message

A concept suggested by philosopher Marshall McLuhan (1911-1980), which states that the media used as the vehicle of delivery more profoundly impacts and affects society than the message it attempts to portray.

125 Tactility

The ability to be physically encountered and experienced through touch.

127 Materiality

Relating to the physical and/or textural quality of the substances used in the production or constitution of an object, thing or artefact.

Activism

139 Marxism
A body of thought based on the political and economic theories of Karl Marx (1818-1883) and Friedrich Engels (1820-1895) consisting of two core interrelated concepts: a critique of the capitalist economy and the summation that the history of all societies can be understood as a class struggle between the proletariat (the working class) and the bourgeoisie (the ruling class).

139 Michel Foucault (1926-1984)
Historian and philosopher interested in how knowledge functions as a form of power, particularly by examining the history of dominant institutions within society, such as hospitals, prisons and psychiatric care facilities, and agreed definitions of illness, mental health and sexuality.

141 Intersectionality

The instance of multiple forms of discrimination, i.e. gender, sexuality, disability, race, age, being in operation simultaneously.

141 Queerness

A challenge to heteronormative societal establishments and ideologies. Queerness is often associated with same sex desire as well as gender and identity politics. Queer theory is a field of critical inquiry concerned with the theorising of queerness, as well as offering queer readings and assessment of texts and cultural phenomena. Philosopher Judith Butler (b. 1956) is a key proponent of the movement.

143 Feminism

Broad grouping of international and historically specific ideologies addressing the oppressions, rights and interests of women. Many branches of feminism exist and coexist with varying concerns and emphasises.

143 Non-binary gender
Individuals who reject being identified according to conventional male or female gender definitions.

143 Propaganda
Images, information, ideas or opinions that lack objectivity with the intent to incite particular emotional responses, sell ideas or goods, further political agenda or promote particular ideologies or causes.

143 Capitalism
An economic system characterised by the production of commodities, private ownership and control of property, business and industry for profit.

149 Utopia

A vision or concept of an ideal society or environment, which can be imaged but never realised in actuality.

153 Neoliberalism
A political ideology and economic system that values and promotes free trade, deregulation of economic markets and private entrepreneurship with an accompanying ideology of individualism.

153 Relational Aesthetics

Term offered by Nicolas Bourriaud (b. 1965) to describe works of art that perform through participatory involvement with audiences, often in social contexts and environments rather than in a gallery setting. Critic Claire Bishop (b. 1971) challenges the ambitions of participatory art and the criteria by which it is judged, positing that a lack of aesthetic criticism has meant that these works are judged on ethical or political terms rather than by artistic or aesthetic standards.

155 Recuperation

Capitalism's ability to absorb and neutralise critique and then represent it with the means to suit its own agenda.

157 Socially engaged practice

Works of art or design that involve communities in action or debate, to raise awareness or improve their local environment. Often, it is associated with activism because it provides an arena for people to have agency in their own lives, and is often politically motivated.

159 Guy Debord (1931-1994)
Philosopher Guy Debord penned *The Society of the Spectacle* (1967), which analyses how consumer driven capitalism supersedes all other forms of social control, like poverty or religion; dissenters are pacified through consumption and individuals are isolated. Debord's theory of 'the commodity spectacle' describes all social relationships as being mediated by images, and a real or authentic society is replaced by mere representation. Debord's ideas can be read as prescient of twenty-first century phenomena like celebrity culture, information technologies and neoliberalism.

159 Détournement
A revision or reworking of a past motif or media so as to have the opposite meaning or message.

163 Consciousness raising
Feminist form of activism, where small, women-only groups discuss and share their personal experiences with the intention of understanding individual experiences as collective ones that are the result of living in a patriarchal society and as such are not the responsibility of the individual.

163 Alienation
Concept devised by Karl Marx (1818-1883) to describe the exclusory, separating and dehumanising effect that capitalism, and more specifically, nineteenth-century industrialised production, had on workers. Long hours, mass production lines and poor wages alienated workers from each other, their work and the goods they produced.

Education

167 Cooperative learning
Students learn by working in groups towards a common goal. By learning cooperatively, students are able to learn from and use each other's skills and knowledge. The teacher facilitates learning rather than just imparting information. Cooperative learning was notably advocated by educator Paulo Freire (1921-1997) in *Pedagogy of the Oppressed* (1968) as a method to counteract the oppression he saw during his experience teaching literacy skills to adults in Brazil.

171 Community of practice
A concept developed by educationalist Étienne Wenger (b. 1952) to describe formal and informal social groups who share a common craft, profession or concern, and therefore can learn together by exchanging knowledge and experiences.

173 Play
Educationalist and inventor of the kindergarten system, Friedrich Fröbel (1782-1852), developed a set of theories that promoted play within early years education. He recognised the importance of encouraging imaginative and creative engagement with materials and the world, particularly for young children.

173 Constructivist learning
The concept of knowledge as constructed, rather than passively acquired, through personal experiences. Meaning is constructed by making connections between new experiences and prior knowledge. Key theorists in this area are Jean Piaget (1896-1980) and Lev Vygotsky (1896-1934); the influential work of educational reformer John Dewey (1859-1952) is thought to form the foundations of constructivist thought.

181 Reflective practice
Critical reflection and analysis of actions and experiences to continuously learn and improve in desired endeavours.

183 Dialogic teaching
Using talk as a learning tool, encouraging discussions between teachers and learners, as well as peers, about their experiences, (mis)understandings and feelings.

187 Experiential learning
A cyclical process involving reflecting on concrete experiences, learning from the experiences in order to identify the appropriate next course of action.

Index

Page numbers in *italic* refer to images.

A
activism 136–63
actors 28
adaptation and interpretation 40–53
    The Bhagavad Gita 50, *50–3*
    Further Feminisms Sketchbook 41, *41–2*
    Memory Palace at The Victoria and Albert Museum 46, *47–9*
    The Picture of Dorian Gray 44, *45*
Ahsan, Hamja 162, *163*
alienation 163
allegory 31
An Alternative Archive of Brutalist Architecture 90, *90–1*
analytical thinking 17
anonymity 18, 148
Anthropocene 81
anthropology 63
Anyango Grünewald, Catherine 54, *54–7*
aura 111
author 45
authorial practices 17
authorless illustration 18
authorship 24–59
autoethnographic illustrators 36–7, *37–9*
autoethnography 29
autonomous practices 17

B
Barnett, Gareth 90, *90–1*, 192, *192*
Barthes Roland 43, 59
The Bauhaus 105
Bear and Me 198, *199*
behaviour, models of 156–7, *157–8*
behaviours in illustrative practice 16
benefits of a research project 213
Berger, John 44
The Bhagavad Gita 50, *50–3*
Bhushan, Anna 50, *50–3*
bias and prejudice 92
Bill Bragg 98, *99–101*
Black Matter 148, *149–52*
Blank Slash 58, *59*
Britton Newell, Laurie 46
Burdock, Christy 178, *179–80*

C
Campaign for Nuclear Disarmament 140
capitalism 143
Carle, Eric 197
Carnec, Marguerite 77, *78–80*
Chandigarh – Concrete and Shadows 67, *68–71*
Cheverton, Ed 171, *171–2*
Clarke, Chris 98, *99–101*
Clifton, Darryl *197–8*
Coe, Sue 77
collaboration 17, 22, 173
    Collaborative Illustrations 171, *171–2*
studio learning and 167–8
collections 126
comedy 140–1, *142*
comics
    Black Matter 148, *149–52*
    World Comics 181–2, *182–3*
community of practice 171
compromises 139, 158
Concrete 110–11, *112–13*
Concrete.RIP 192, *192*
Conrad, Joseph 54, *54–7*
consciousness raising 163
consent forms 214, 215
constructivist learning 173
context 17, 19, 114
cooperative learning 167
Copsey, Laura 127–8, *129–30*
craft-based skills 104
crafting 102–35
Crivelli's Garden (The Visitation) 178
Crossing Time 122, *123*
The Curious Case of Mavis Davis 156–7, *157–8*

D
data visualisation 189–92
    Concrete.RIP 192, *192*
    Dear Data 189, *190–1*
Davies, Rebecca 156–7, *157–8*
Dear Data 189, *190–1*
'Death of the Author' 43, 59
Debord, Guy 159
Debris and Phenomena 84, *85–6*
decolonising movement 101
definitions 14
dérive 90, 91
détournement 140, 159
diagrammatic and instructional illustrations 193, *194–6*
Dialectograms 87, *88–9*
dialogic teaching 183
dialogues 168
discipline of illustration 14–18
display mapping, inspirational 168, *169–70*

Don't Believe the Papers 64, *65–6*
Ducker, Kate 124, *124–5*

E editorial illustration 97–8, *99–101*
education 164–201
educational space 167
Elsewhere 186, *187–8*
ethics 213–15
ethnocentrism 97, 213
ethnography 69
event, illustration as 152–3, *154–5*
events 27
expanded practice 17–18
experience, documents of 181–5
    Probably Nothing 181, *184–5*
    World Comics 181–2, *182–3*
experiential learning 187, 197, 198

F fabrication 126–8, *129–30*
fabular 26–7
Fallon Mc Guigan, Ruairi 36–7, *37–9*
Fauchon, Mireille 64, *65–6*
feminism 143
feminist zines 140
Flanagan's Bar 36–7, *37–9*
flâneur / flâneuse 87
focalisation 27–8
Foucault, Michel 139
The Foundling Museum 174, *175*
Four Corners Books 44
Further Feminisms Sketchbook 41, *41–2*
Fusco, Leah 92–3, *93–6*
future visions 148, *149–52*

G Gannon, Rachel 67, *68–71*
Giant Digestive System 200, *201*
Gliddon, Katie 64
Goodwin, Amy 107–8, *109*
Google Maps 90
Green Belt Properties: Costing a House 153, *154–5*
Greenberg, Isobel 46
Greenwood, James 186
group working 209–10
Guantánamo Diary 98, *99–101*

H Halls, Jon 153, *154–5*
Harry, Emma 81, *82–3*
Heart of Darkness 54, *54–7*
helping existing organisations 158–63
    Shy Radicals 162, *163*
    The Visual Imaginary 158–9, *160–1*
Heritage as Process 174, *175*
Holtom, Gerald 139–40

House of Illustration 122, 176
    House of Illustration Residency 178, *179–80*
how to do research 64, *65–6*
humour 140–1, *142*
Hunter, Rob 46

I *I am a mess, but so are you. Love, Utopia* 105, *106*
idea development 104, 168
identity 15, 92, 143, *144–7*
Illich, Ivan 167
illustration and research 18–22
Illustration Futures 204–5
illustration-based research 186, *187–8*
illustrative writing 58, *59*
image research 31–2, 53, *54–7*
imagination, making meaning with 31
immaterial technologies 131–5
    Shhh! at Tate Britain 131, *131–3*
    At Some Point, This Tree Will Fall 134, *135*
The In-Between: An Ode to Epping Forest 116, *117–20*
informed
    consent 214–15
    practice 139
instructional and diagrammatic illustrations 193, *194–6*
interactive drawing experience 46
interactive illustration 197–201
    Bear and Me 198, *199*
    Giant Digestive System 200, *201*
intersectionality 139, 141
interviews 72, 73, 210–12

J Johnston, Katie Rose 200, *201*
Jones, Gareth 44, *45*
Jones, Lily 41, *41–2*
Jost, Emily 176, *177*
'The Jungle' refugee camp 77, *78–80*

K Katt, Serena 31–2, *33–5*
Kaur, Jasleen 114, *115*, *169*
Keating, Marianne 74, *74–6*
Kelly, Johnny 46
key ideas 216–19
Kunzru, Hari 46

L *Landlessness* 74, *74–6*
Langford, Sarah 193, *194–6*
language 15, 121
Latin Elephant 158–9
Layered Time 81, *82–3*
Le Corbusier 67
learning through illustration 176, *177*
legacies 213–14

APPENDIX

Index

L

Lemm, David 84, *85–6*
Lieu de Vie 77, *78–80*
life
    drawing from 67, *68–71*
    stories 30
lifeworld 39
    multisensory 81, *82–3*
Lillie, Rachel 116, *117–20, 170*
linguistic turn 43
listening 72–4, *74–6*
Lizzie: Striding Along 107–8, *109*
Lupi, Giorgia 189, *190–1*

M

making-based research 168
Man, Charlene 200, *201*
mapping, inspirational display 168, *169–70*
mark-making 105, *106*
Marxism 139
materiality 127
materials, meaning of 110–11, *112–13*
McManus, Esther 186, *187–8*
me, you and everyone else 92–3, *93–6*
mediated objects 122
medical practitioners 181
medium is the message 115
meetings 209–10
memes 147–8
Memory Palace at The Victoria and Albert Museum 46, *47–9*
metaphors 27, 43, 58, *59*
methodology 15, 19
methods 15, 19
    framework for catergorising research 20
Miller, Mitch 87, *88–9*
models
    of behaviour 156–7, *157–8*
    of practice 8–9, *10–11*
Modern Gods 46, *47–9*
Molloy, Paddy 122, *123*
multisensory lifeworld 81, *82–3*

N

narrative
    components 26–9
    inquiries 29–32, *33–5*
    text 26
narratology 26, 27
narrators 27, 36
Neal, Ben 192, *192*
neoliberalism 153
news reporting 97–8, *99–101*
Nexus Studios 46
Nightingale, Phoebe 58, *59*
non-binary gender 143
Nordin, Rose 162, *163*
Northeye 92–3, *93–6*

O

Oasis Social Club 156, *157–8*
objectivity 21, 92
objects 114–20
    illustrated 126
    The In-Between: An Ode to Epping Forest 116, *117–20*
    Tools for Living 114, *115*
objects, 3d, physical and virtual forms, illustration as 121–5
    Crossing Time 122, *123*
    Special Bodily Sensations 124, *124–5*
observation 67, 76–7, *78–80*
originality 22
othering 99

P

paratext 29
'the personal is political' 138
Peterson, Lina *169*
philosophy of education 166
The Picture of Dorian Gray 44, *45*
picture visual research 31–2, 53, *54–7*
planning and preparation, research 62–3
play 173, 198
Play_Learn 197–8
    Bear and Me 198, *199*
    Play-O-Logy Giant Digestive System 200, *201*
politics 138
Posavec, Stefanie 46, 189, *190–1*
positioning 92, 213
power play 138–9
prejudice and bias 92
Princess May Primary School 176, *177*
principles of illustration practice 16–17
Probably Nothing 181, *184–5*
process, illustration as 14–15
propaganda 143
proposals 208–9
protest, visual identity of 139–40
psychogeography 84, 87, 91
Purcell, Alexander 98, *99–101*

Q

qualitative research 23, 29
queerness 141

R

reading, skill of 40
recognisability 18
recuperation 155
reflective
    journals 212
    practice 181, 212
Rego, Paula 178

relational aesthetics 153
reliability, language of 193, *194–6*
reporter, illustrator as 62
reporting 60–101
research and illustration 18–22
residencies, illustration 178, *179–80*, 205
response, interpretations and 43
responsible practice 213–15
Ridley Road Market 176, *177*
rigorous practice 20–1
at risk groups, working with 214
Risograph printer 107
role, expanded 17–18
Rowe, Daise 110–11, *112–13*

S Sachs, Jack 131, *131–3*
Salazar, Ligaya 46
satirical imagery 141
From Scratch 127–8, *129–30*
semiotics 53
sequences 28
Sharma, Sharad 181–2, *182–3*
Shhh! at Tate Britain 131, *131–3*
Shy Radicals 162, *163*
signature pedagogies 167–72
    Collaborative Illustrations 171, *171–2*
    Studio Walls 168, *169–70*
signwriting 107–8, *109*
Sims, Cat 148, *149–52*
sketchbooks 72
social justice, supporting 158–63
    Shy Radicals 162, *163*
    The Visual Imaginary 158–9, *160–1*
social practice 19
socially engaged practice 157
At Some Point, This Tree Will Fall 134, *135*
Sordini, Sandra 105, *106*
space, education 167
Special Bodily Sensations 124, *124–5*
Stitz, Angelo 9, *10–11*
stories 27
    life 30
    unfolding 30
    unstable realities 30–1
storytelling 26, 29–30
storyworlds 28–9
strategies
    illustration practice 16
    research 64
studio learning and collaboration 167–8, 171, *171–2*
Studio Walls 168, *169–70*

stuff of life 114–20
    The In-Between: An Ode to Epping Forest 116, *117–20*
    Tools for Living 114, *115*
subjectivity 19
Sunday's Child 31–2, *33–5*

T tactility 121, 125
tangibility 107
Taylor, Rachel Emily 174, *175*
terminology 15
Tomos, Sion Ap 176, *177*
tools
    and instruments 17
    of the trade 107–8, *109*
Tools for Living 114, *115*
touch 121
Towndrow, Lizzie Scarlett 198, *199*
Translational Type 9, *10–11*
Tristram, Matilda 181, *184–5*
truth 97
Twist, Olivia 143, *144–7*
typeface 9, *10–11*

U utopia 149

V *The Very Hungry Caterpillar* 197
visibility 18
The Visual Imaginary 158–9, *160–1*
Visualising Invisible Oceanic Landscapes 193, *194–6*
Vormittag, Luise 158–9, *160–1*

W walking 84–91
    An Alternative Archive of Brutalist Architecture 90, *90–1*
    Debris and Phenomena 84, *85–6*
    Dialectograms 87, *88–9*
Ward, Colin 167
Ways of Seeing 44
White, Nick 171, *171–2*
who do you think I am? 143, *144–7*
Wild, Jack 134, *135*
Wilde, Oscar 44, *45*
Winston, Sam 46, *47–9*
Women's March, 2017 141, *142*
working with others 209–10
workshops 84, 159, 173–4, 193, 198
    Heritage as Process 174, *175*
    Ridley Road Market 176, *177*
World Comics 181–2, *182–3*
writing, illustrative 58, *59*

Acknowledgements

For Jude Brown and Robert 'Bob' Fauchon

We would like to thank the following in particular for their encouragement and support developing this project: Olivia Ahmad, Gareth Barnett, Holly Birtles, Stephanie Black, Myles Brown, Sheena Calvert, Darryl Clifton, Debbie Cook, Laura Copsey, Jane Cradock-Watson, Lotte Crawford, Polona Dolžan, Noel Douglas, Elmira 'Bolly' Fauchon, Theresa Ferrier, Four Corners Books, Leah Fusco, Geoffrey Grandfield, Maggie Gray, Jaleen Grove, Jon Halls, Arjun Harrison-Mann, Emma Harry, India Harvey, Maria Kapajeva, Jasleen Kaur, Fran Lloyd, Lainy Malkani, Paul Micklethwaite, Desdemona McCannon, Martin McGrath, Esther McManus, Rosy Nicholas, Ima-Abasi Okon, Lina Peterson, Rabbit Road Press, Richard Roberts, Daise Rowe, Ligaya Salazar, Amanda Schiff, Angelo Stitz, James 'Jim' Walker, Nick White, Jack Wild and Luise Vormittag.

We are very grateful to the contributing artists and designers for so generously sharing their images, ideas and knowledge.

A special thank you to the students and staff at Kingston School of Art, Royal College of Art, Camberwell College of Arts, University of Bedfordshire and UCA Farnham who are, and have been, a constant source of inspiration for us over the years.